The Reselection

The Reselection of MPs

Alison Young

 Heinemann Educational Books · London

Heinemann Educational Books Ltd
22 Bedford Square, London WC1B 3HH
LONDON EDINBURGH MELBOURNE AUCKLAND
HONG KONG SINGAPORE KUALA LUMPUR NEW DELHI
IBADAN NAIROBI JOHANNESBURG
EXETER (NH) KINGSTON PORT OF SPAIN

ISBN 0 435 83371 5

Phototypesetting by Georgia Origination, Liverpool
Printed in Great Britain by Biddles Ltd, Guildford, Surrey

Contents

Acknowledgements

This book started life as a thesis for the degree of M.Phil. at Sheffield University. I am grateful to Professor Stuart Walkland, my supervisor, in the Department of Political Theory and Institutions, for his advice and encouragement, without which publication would never have been achieved. I would also like to thank Patrick Seyd for guidance in the preparatory stages, and particularly for help and advice on the research for Chapter 7. Those members of the Labour party who agreed to be interviewed about the Brightside case gave generously of their time and knowledge, and received me with great kindness. Jonathan Foster of the Sheffield *Morning Telegraph* and Michael Cooke also made helpful contributions to that part of the study. Francis Hawkings commented meticulously, and valuably, on the first draft. Christine Pickard, Pat Carpenter and Sue Parker have typed successive drafts. I am indebted to all of them, as well as to all those friends, too numerous to mention by name, who have helped in many other ways. They all have my thanks. Most of all, however, my gratitude is due to my husband, Charles Young, not only for much valuable criticism, but also for his unfailing encouragement and support.

Alison Young
January 1983

1 The contemporary context: the changing face of British politics

The recently successful campaign to make the reselection of Labour MPs mandatory before each election has been portrayed as a new threat to the independence of Members of Parliament. Fears have been expressed that small groups of militants will exercise an influence out of all proportion to their numbers, and use a change in the party's democratic processes to further their own political ends. In February 1982, when four MPs had failed to get through the new reselection process, Roy Hattersley said:

> Hard working and devoted Members of Parliament have been dismissed without reason or warning. There have been purges of moderates on general committees and pogroms against delegates who listened to their consciences and obeyed their mandates, but offended the prejudices of little tightly organised sects. (*Sunday Times*, 14 February 1982)

But there is nothing new in this. More than a century ago, W. E. Forster, MP for Bradford, and as Gladstone's Minister for Education responsible for the 1870 Education Act, which had aroused strong hostility among Nonconformists, found his reselection as Liberal candidate threatened by the newly formed party caucus in the town. He would be put forward as the candidate only if he agreed to be bound by the decision of the caucus. Forster protested vigorously, arguing that this would prevent him from appealing to his constituents, or indeed to the party. The chairman of the party, described as a 'militant', replied that 'a candidate had no right to appeal to the whole constituency; that he owed obedience to the party and its committee'. Forster finally agreed after a minor change of wording in the organisation's statutes and survived as an MP.

This is one of two examples cited by Ostrogorski in his seminal study *Democracy and the Organisation of Political Parties*, first published in 1902. Though with hindsight it is clear that Ostrogorski seriously overestimated the influence of the caucus[1] and in any case deeply distrusted the idea of political parties,[2] his analysis has a direct relevance to developments in the Labour Party since 1970.

Three separate comparisons may be made between Ostrogorski's findings and the state of the Labour Party today. First, Labour conferences have repeatedly charged the party's leadership with being out of touch with the grassroots of the party and indeed with the electorate in general. This same accusation was levelled against the Liberal Party, split between Whigs and Radicals, at the end of the nineteenth century. The Whig leadership, Ostrogorski wrote,

> received notice to quit, they had held their position only too long; they had been, they were told, simply a clique engaged in the selfish pursuit of power, they were out of sympathy with all the aspirations of the nation ... as the leaders were moderates, both were confounded in one common reprobation (p. 94).

Secondly, opponents of the Campaign for Labour Party Democracy, which was the chief motivating force behind the reselection campaign, have accused it, as the quotation from Roy Hattersley shows, of being a small unrepresentative group, using the battle cry of democracy to conceal their true intentions. Ostrogorski took the same view of the nineteenth-century party organisations:

> The Caucus, which rallied round it the advanced and ardent spirits of the party, soon became the stronghold of a faction imbued with a sectarian spirit and all the more intolerant and imperious because the popular form of its constitution gave it a pretext for putting itself forward as the only true legitimate representative of the Liberal Party (p. 95).

Again, Ostrogorski's strictures on the relationship between the local party and the Member are strikingly similar to some made today. The local activists, he wrote, have already assured themselves of the candidate's political orthodoxy, but this is not enough; 'they scrutinize his votes, they weigh his words', and generally 'keep him up to the mark' by passing resolutions. '... having lent him their moral resources, they consider themselves entitled to a mortgage over his conscience' (1964 p. 229). In 1981 Harold Lever expressed similar views; he wrote that the new reselection procedure was designed to

> place a continuous threat over every Member to induce his conformity to the detailed wishes of his local committee. Before, they could

---

[1]See Lipset's introduction to Ostrogorski.
[2]One commentator described Ostrogorski's book as 'pervaded by preconceived hostility' (Garvin quoted by McKenzie, p. 6).

argue but the Member decided. Now he must toe the line or be thrown out.... Local Labour Party caucuses are becoming increasingly arrogant and aggressive in the deployment of their new powers. ('Accountability', *London Review of Books*, 19 March–1 April 1981.)

It is with the relationship between the MP and his constituency and his local party organisation that this book will be chiefly concerned. Two aspects of the relationship, related but separate, will be the theme of what follows. First is the question of who should choose or reselect the candidate: the party activists, its members, or the voters at large? Second is the issue of which, if any, of these three layers of constituents, or some other body, such as the party conference, should influence the MP's votes and public attitudes on current political issues? There is no simple, unambiguous answer to these complex questions. The nature of representation itself, as will be shown in Chapter 2, is fraught with complications. It has been for centuries a subject of debate, not only in academic circles, but also in the political arena, and occasionally in the wider public domain as well. The successful campaign in the Labour Party for the automatic reselection of MPs has brought it once more to the forefront of political debate. And it is not only the position of MPs which is being challenged; at the same time numerous other important aspects of the British political system are being questioned or have already been subjected to change.

The debate on representation is conducted in very dated terms. Political practice has moved ahead of representative theory. The developments of the late nineteenth and twentieth centuries – the extension of the franchise, the growth of the mass party, and of strict party discipline, the enormous extension of government activity, and the concomitant growth of corporate power – were not, with the exception of the first, foreseen by the nineteenth-century reformers, and certainly not by Burke, whose formulation of the proper role of an MP became a central strand in the unwritten British constitution. As Eulau wrote in a more wide-ranging study:

Our contemporary real life problems are such that none of the traditional formulations of representation are relevant to the solution of the representational problems which the modern polity faces. (Quoted by Birch, 1972 p. 103.)

Eulau was considering the application of representational theory in a variety of contexts; the scope of this book is much narrower, but nonetheless it can be seen that the Burkean paradigm of an independent trustee does not fit comfortably with the modern British political system. Politics, in what Samuel Beer has characterised as the Collectivist era, combines party government with giving a large role to group interests. These are far better organised than they were in the nineteenth century, the heyday of individualism, but the notion of functional representation has a long history. 'It was present in Burke's general view of society, as well as his idea of representation, and went back to Tudor and medieval times.' (Beer, 1965, p. 18.) In the modern age, Beer discerns in the managed economy and the welfare state two sets of interlocking relationships. One chain is representative in nature: consumer groups exert inflence on the government and parties bid for the consumers' votes. The other is functional; the government bargains with producer groups for cooperation. Government needs these groups for 'advice, acquiescence and approval', a far cry from the Benthamite fear of sinister interests, and a model allowing little or no scope for the independence of individual Members of Parliament.

The major part of Beer's study was written in the early 1960s. Since then functional institutions of all kinds have proliferated and fears have been expressed about the advance of the corporate state. One writer notices in the 1960s a change from an essentially pluralist to a fundamentally corporatist system of functional representation. The tripartism of both Conservative and Labour governments in the 1970s, plus Britain's continuing economic crisis, led to a 'powerful movement towards incorporation' (Smith, 1979, p. 163). 'Governments wanted increasingly to co-opt the main pressure groups into collaborating in economic policy-making, partly out of desperation, partly as a risk-spreading device.' Smith fears that functional representation is a threat to our system of representative government, and that what we are faced with is a return to something like the medieval system, a 'new court politics' (p. 179). This may be rather an exaggerated view, but the corporatist tendency of modern government can nonetheless be argued to threaten the political equality of the individual. Another writer (Harrison, 1980, p. 189) who fears the effect of the corporatist drift on the individual argues that one important line of defence is the political party, which can provide a means of expressing a wide range of views and opinions (p. 113).

Parties are not recognised by the unwritten British constitution, but they are vital to the system of representative government which has evolved over the last one hundred and fifty years. Although the parties are as much a focus for the dissatisfaction with British politics as any other institution, they remain a necessary and important part of British government today.

First, they have a role in the mobilisation of consent; this is thought necessary even in totalitarian states which have only one party, 'to mobilise consent or coerce compliance' (R. Rose, 1976, p. 467). Secondly, parties play, or should play, a role in aggregating and ordering the demands of the electorate. They can generalise where interest groups cannot. British parties have tended, especially during the period of consensus politics in the 1950s and 1960s, to perform this function rather too well, at the expense of their third function, the articulation of interests. Consensus pushed minority groups away from the main parties, and into single issue pressure groups, which increased enormously in numbers in the 1960s.

Ostrogorski thought that single issue parties would moderate the domination of the caucus. Recent experience has not borne this out, but in any case he saw party as inherently corrupting and undemocratic, and democracy as an individual, atomised activity. Such individualism, as R. H. S. Crossman pointed out, could be nothing less than disastrous (1963, p. 14). Single issue politics and the consequent fragmentation of political life is another indication of the loss of faith in traditional political institutions. The corrective to what Wolin has called 'the fetish of groupism' (1961, pp. 433–4) is a reassertion of a general political dimension.

Fourthly, political parties represent a commitment to the system, something which much corporate and pluralist activity cannot do. These functions cannot well be performed by other means. Thus, parties remain necessary, despite their imperfections. These faults have been pointed out by Nevil Johnson. Arguing that parties in Britain have much less impact than they do in most other European countries, he says they 'resemble fragments of a thin pie-crust, floating on the social stew' (1977, p. 168). In spite of this,

> they remain the indispensable means by which people are enabled to choose representatives, to display their preferences for men and policies and to bring into existence a political will directed to the tasks of government (p. 217).

Parties, however, 'are not passive translators of individual preferences into instructions to office-holders' (Rose, 1977, p. xix), rather as Ostrogorski saw them 'powerful instruments for dominating the electorate, for imposing officials, opinions and policies on the public' (Lipset's introduction to Ostrogorski, 1964, p. lvii). With the development of a strong party system, the question that is decided at a general election is what kind of government the electors want, rather than who is to represent them in Parliament. Nevertheless, the personality and political views of MPs do matter, especially to their local parties, and the late 1960s and 1970s saw an increase in the number of disputes between MPs and constituency parties, especially in the Labour Party. Several of these will be studied in detail in later chapters. There is frequently a variety of reasons for such disputes and each case has its own special character, but there is usually some dissatisfaction with the MP, often going back some years, which can be acted upon if unusual circumstances arise or changes take place within the local party. The 'prickly individualist' may easily fall foul of his local party, especially if he strays too far towards the centre of the political spectrum, or has a less than conventional private life. A dismissal attempt may be triggered off by some action of the MP himself, or the coming into prominence of an important issue, such as the Suez crisis or entry to the EEC. A successful dismissal attempt may depend on 'widening the scope' of the dispute (See Dickson, 1975); in a number of these cases, the MP has found himself facing a wide range of charges.

Recent Labour party disputes, however, show something more than this: the increasing dissatisfaction of the left wing of the party with the leadership. Two changes were made in the party constitution to cope with this. In 1973 the 'proscribed list' was abolished, which led to the addition to the party of people who had previously been excluded, a move which was later to result in concern in some quarters about 'infiltration' of local parties. Secondly, the rules for the dismissal of an MP were altered so as to make the NEC's role in cases of appeal merely a procedural one, thus making it easier for a local party to get rid of its MP. By the end of the 1970s, in the wake of the Prentice affair, there was enough concern over the activities of extreme left-wingers for two appeals – those of Neville Sandelson and Maureen Colquhoun – to be upheld, though the imminence of a general election may have had something to do with this. In spite of fears about the actions of such groups as the Militant Tendency, by the end of the 1970s the party was a more left-wing one, not only in the constituencies, where the CLPD had succeeded in orchestrating grassroots discontent, but also at the level of the National Executive Committee. No longer could it be said as it had been in the 1960s,

> In the activities of the organisation subcommittee the right-wing heart of the party beats loud and strong. (Paterson, 1967, p. 41.)

In these circumstances, with both the dominant faction on the Executive Committee and the prevailing mood in the constituency parties being distrustful of the leadership and its policies, the Parliamentary Labour Party became the focus of grassroots anger and frustration.

The course of the campaign for reselection will be charted in Chapter 8, but the key point at issue remains not the details of a reselection process, automatic or otherwise, but the question of who the MP represents. Does he represent the local activists or the voters? 'Is he to be a lapdog for a few or a watchdog for all the people?' as one Conservative MP, Patrick Wolridge-Gordon, rather subjectively but revealingly put it in 1962 when he was victorious in a dispute with his local party (quoted by Ranney, 1965 p. 75).

This conflict is perennial and unavoidable, inherent in the system. The problem it poses for conscientious MPs was shown up in the prolonged debate on EEC entry; many MPs on both sides of the House, and both sides of the argument, held 'referenda' in their constituencies in order to ascertain the views of the electorate. Recent Labour Party disputes have sharpened this old conflict, and revived the fears of the excessive power of the caucus. One authority, David Butler, who had previously held firmly to the view that disputes between MPs and their constituency parties were caused principally by personal differences and difficulties in the over-whelming majority of such cases, appears to have moderated his view; political reasons, he now concedes, appear to play a larger part (Butler and Kavanagh, 1980, p. 280). It is certainly true, and not only in constit-uencies where disputes have become public, that local Labour Party activ-ists no longer accept that their role is merely a sustaining one. They want MPs and councillors to be more accountable to them. But what is more important for the party as a whole, and for British politics generally, is the yawning gulf between activists, voters and MPs, a gulf of which the disputes referred to above are but a single manifestation.

The gulf is partly about policy. On main issues, there is no clear majority opinion within the party, as Richard Rose found in 1976. Party cohesion on important issues was very low; Rose's index of intra-party cohesion showed a figure of 25 per cent for Labour voters, compared with 41 per cent for Conservatives (Rose 1976, p. 301). In fact, Labour voters were more likely to agree with Conservative MPs than Labour ones on policy. The gap between the policies set out in the manifesto and the policy preferences of Labour voters was even greater.

> The increasingly self-confident socialism of the Labour Party's activ-ists is in conflict, on the one hand, with the ideas of the parliamentary party and, on the other hand, with the ideas of the electorate. Even the more tepidly socialist ideas of the PLP are too much for the elect-orate. (Drucker, 1979, p. 115.)

Activists, for their part, have a poor opinion of many MPs. For example, at Labour's 1981 Wembley conference, called to decide the question of the method of electing the leader, speaker after speaker was less than polite about the PLP. One said in so many words that the debate was about how much less power the parliamentary party should have. They had voted Reg Prentice to the top of the Shadow Cabinet poll in 1976 – a man who shortly afterwards joined the Conservative Party – and in 1980 had failed to vote Tony Benn onto the committee at all. Another speaker could not accept that MPs knew better than he did, and a third demanded that the 'deep feeling of dissatisfaction in the constituencies' should be heeded.

The drastic fall in individual membership of the Labour Party (from about 600,000 in 1964 to half that figure in 1970, and approximately 250,000 at the time of writing) is partly responsible for this gap in attitudes. The new members who are recruited are usually young energetic and left-wing, while the older more moderate members are often inactive. The young place democracy above job security for MPs in their priorities . The composition of the parliamentary party has changed only slowly over the years, and many of its members have abandoned the old Labour Party ethos to which local parties still partly subscribe (Drucker, 1979, p. 112). The campaign for automatic reselection and for altering the method of the election of the leader of the party, both now successful, have therefore been powerful forces working against the cohesion of the party; this cohesion, Austin Ranney's *Pathways to Parliament* (1965) found in the late 1950s, was provided mainly by the activists in the constituencies. And if proof had been needed that the party had lost much of that cohesion, it was provided by the early successes of the new Social Democratic Party.

These changes, however, should not be seen in isolation; the cohesion of British politics and British social life as a whole has been markedly reduced since Ranney wrote, and many traditional assumptions about the British political system are no longer tenable.

> During the 1970s the established rules of British government were not in the main changed. But almost all of them came under challenge and some were significantly modified. (Butler and Kavanagh, 1980 p. 7.)

Constitutional changes in the last ten or fifteen years have altered the whole context of the debate on representation, and indeed on the British constitution itself. One illuminating way of demonstrating this is to compare some of the key points of A. H. Birch's penetrating 1964 study *Representative and Responsible Government* with constitutional practice today. This study pointed out many of the myths of the constitution as applied to contemporary political practice. In his conclusions, Birch argued that there was no single theory of political representation which commanded general acceptance. 'Instead there is a continuing debate in which a variety of theories are invoked...' (p. 227). Nevertheless, the debate had definable limits. These limits he set out, and it is striking how many of them no longer hold true. First,

> there has been no support in this country for the populist doctrine that representation is an inferior alternative to direct democracy.

A decline in respect for the results of elections and a greater readiness to resort to direct action were both noticeable in the 1970s and will be mentioned later. Secondly,

> No serious politician has suggested that representatives should be bound by specific instructions from their constituents.

Automatic reselection in the Labour Party, now a fact, has brought this nearer than might have been expected even five years ago. Thirdly,

> it has occasionally been proposed that a referendum might be held on a particular issue, but the proposals do not ever appear to have been taken seriously.[1]

Referenda have been held on the EEC and on devolution in Scotland and Wales, as well as on the border issue in Northern Ireland. So the referendum is now one of the instruments open to governments for dealing with contentious issues.

The other limits set out by Birch have not been so noticeably broken down. A one-party system has not been seriously suggested, though after the election of the Thatcher government in 1979, there was some talk of extending the life of parliaments, and many were alarmed by Tony Benn's speech at the 1980 Labour Party conference when he spoke of creating one thousand peers overnight. The electoral system, on the other hand, has been brought into question and there has been some debate on the desirability of primary elections, a subject which will be discussed in Chapter 10. In addition controversies over communal representation, unknown fifteen years ago, have become a live issue in Northern Ireland, where several attempts have been made to give the Roman Catholic minority more effective representation, and the electoral system is now one of proportional representation, except for Westminster elections.

There are several more assumptions, quite valid in 1964, which can not be taken for granted in the 1980s. Noting the blurring of class conflict, and indeed of political conflict in general in the post-war years, both of which are now sharper once more, Birch wrote:

> Nobody now thinks, as Laski and Cripps did in the thirties, that the system might be drastically amended if the Labour Party were to win the next election.

With Labour now committed to withdrawal from the Common Market, the renunciation of nuclear weapons and the alternative economic strategy, this is no longer the case. Again,

> Another and most important tradition of British political behaviour is the tradition that the government of the day should be given all the powers it needs to carry out its policy. The parliamentary opposition does not normally make any attempt to obstruct legislation ... or reduce the financial appropriations for which the government asks.

---

[1]These quotations are all from Chapter 17 of *Representative and Responsible Government* (1964). Birch himself has made similar points in subsequent publications.

Although this is still broadly true (see Richard Rose, 1980, Chapter 4), the experience of the 1974–9 Labour Government showed that this tradition is no longer always operative. Other traditions have been eroded too; collective cabinet responsibility was waived in 1975 over the EEC issue for the first time since 1932.

Thus constitutional practice has changed in a variety of ways. The 'rules of the game' have altered (see Dennis Kavanagh, 1978), and the old bases of thinking about the British political system are no longer secure. The changes that have taken place in recent years are of three kinds. First, institutional changes in recent years render the nineteenth century formulation of the constitution still more out of date. The Liberal theory of the Constitution – with parliamentary sovereignty and ministerial accountability as its two main pillars – has passed through three main phases. Starting as a programme of reform, it became an idealised version of reality, and then gradually 'a set of traditional principles to which practice no longer corresponds' (Birch, 1964, p. 66). But if parliamentary sovereignty, in a political rather than a strictly legal sense, was a constitutional fiction in 1964, it is now plainly a falsehood. Developments since then have further eroded parliamentary power.

The accession of the United Kingdom to the European Economic Community has made British law subject to European law on a range of subjects. Direct elections to the European Parliament detract further from the position of individual MPs and indeed the parliamentary parties at Westminster. The proposals for devolving some power to Scotland and Wales by introducing elected assemblies, and the holding of referenda on this as well as on the Common Market issue, are also major constitutional departures, which reduce the status and actual political impact of the House of Commons. More generally, and more gradually, major groups outside government and Parliament have played an increasing role in policy-making, at least till the 1979 general election. One example is the Social Contract, which linked agreement on wages with advances in social benefits. Thus governments have had to make their policy in consultation with the trade unions, the corporations, the regions and the EEC (see Ionescu, 1975a and b) and 'the number of dependency relationships in which government is involved has increased substantially' (King, 1975).

In addition to institutional changes, some gradual and some more rapid, shifts in attitudes over the last fifteen or so years have been significant. This is no doubt partly a consequence of the failure of successive governments to live up to public expectations, expectations inspired largely by the political parties themselves. But by the end of the 1960s, there was a distaste for the remoteness of government, coupled with a desire for greater participation, though not in the established parties.

During the post-war years, political scientists had developed theories of 'representative democracy' which purported to be a value-free and accurate description of how western democracies operated. First formulated by Schumpeter in the 1940s, and dubbed 'equilibrium democracy' by Macpherson, the model represented a system in which competing parties vied for the votes of the electorate. The role of the citizen was reduced to a minimum and some theorists even discerned a positive function for the stability of the system in limited participation and apathy (see Pateman, 1970, Chapter 1). By the end of the 1960s, this model no longer seemed to be adequate. Though the idea of participatory democracy has had less impact in the United Kingdom than in America, it is worth quoting one American analysis of its ideas:

> There is a repugnance towards being administered, or manipulated, and not only that, but a repugnance towards being governed; and beyond that a repugnance towards being represented. (George Kateb in Pennock and Chapman (eds.), 1975.)

This feeling includes a strong desire for greater equality; few in Britain would express themselves so strongly, but there has been the development of 'political impatience' (see Birch, 1980, p. 174), in place of a liking for being governed which was discernible in 1964 (Birch, 1964, p. 245),

> ....within a generation Britain had changed from being a rather relaxed society to being a rather tense one, and from being a society that was relatively easy to govern to being one which is increasingly difficult to govern (Birch, 1980, 4th edn. p. 269).

Not only is society more tense, but ideological cleavages are more distinct, and elections are no longer such a strong legitimising device as they once were. There is a greater tendency to challenge the decisions of Parliament, as witnessed by the campaigns against the 1971 Industrial Relations Act and the 1972 Housing Finance Act, which culminated in the long drawn out battle at Clay Cross.

An increasing tendency to resort to direct action may be seen in other spheres; this trend is often seen as illegitimate, as representing 'values which have little time for the autonomy of Parliament' (Kavanagh, 1978, p. 10). But, like functional representation, direct action has a long pedigree. As Ostrogorski pointed out, three great reforms – religious, parliamentary and economic (the Corn Laws) – were 'obtained under pressure from extra-constitutional organisations' (Ostrogorski, 1964, p. 68 and see also Wootton in Gwyn and Rose (eds.) 1980), and not without serious disruption. Left-wingers today have not failed to point this out; for example, Tony Benn in a 1970 Fabian pamphlet,

> Change from below, the formulation of demands from the populace to end unacceptable injustice, supported by direct action, has played

a far larger part in shaping British democracy than most constitutional lawyers, political commentators, historians or statesmen
have ever cared to admit.

He went on to argue that citizens were demanding more power and should
have it.

> The British parliament cannot expect to be exempted from this
> general demand for greater participation ... the next stage in public
> participation in government is bound to come from the first serious
> reconsideration of the possibility of adding some direct decision-
> making ... (1970, pp. 19 and 23).

A third major type of change that has taken place is in the two-party
system, which was seen in the 1950s and 1960s as immutable and a basic
reason for the satisfactory nature of the British system. As with the
doctrine of Parliamentary sovereignty, this is a constitutional myth based
on relatively short experience; for a short time at the end of the nineteenth
century, and again since 1935. The fragmentation of the stable system of
two main parties taking turns at Government has been fairly slow. At the
end of the 1960s, there was the experience of Scottish and Welsh Nationalist by-election victories, and student unrest. The victory of the Conservatives, led by Edward Heath, in the 1970 general election marked the
beginning of an era of greater political bitterness and polarisation as well
as the height of the great EEC debate, and increasing dissatisfaction
among Labour activists. In terms of election results, however, the
changing face of British politics was not really clear until February 1974
when Heath called an election on the issue of 'who runs Britain?'

But the decline in support for the two main parties can be traced back
much further than this. In 1951, the two main parties received more than
96 per cent of the total vote at the general election. At successive general
elections the turn-out fell and the percentage of votes gained by Labour
and Conservatives also declined. In 1970, a turn-out of only 72 per cent
gave less than 90 per cent of the total vote to the two main parties. In 1974,
there was a major break in the figures; although the turn-out rose to nearly
79 per cent, what was most marked was the fall in support for the two main
parties, both in voting figures and in seats in the House of Commons.
Together they received only 75 per cent of the votes. Thirty-seven MPs
(compared with seven in 1959) belonged to minor parties; Northern Irish
MPs were no longer included with the Conservatives. It was the first post-
war election which gave no clear-cut result. Edward Heath's negotiations
with the Liberal Party came to nothing, so Labour formed the government. The Liberal leader, Jeremy Thorpe, remarked in the House a few
days later:

Looking around the House, one realises that we are all minorities now – indeed some more than others (Hansard, HC 1974, vol. 870, col. 13).

The second general election of 1974 produced the same share of the vote for the two major parties, though Labour had, temporarily at least, a majority of seats. It was already clear, however, that the system which once, while being unfair to minorities, produced stable one-party government, 'no longer had the saving grace of manufacturing clear majorities' (Kavanagh, 1978, p. 16). For Labour, especially, the results of the past few elections were discouraging. It had lost the 1951 election with 49 per cent of the popular vote; it won the October 1974 election with little more than 39 per cent, less than at any time since 1935. Nor had the Conservatives any cause for cheer; their percentage of the vote fell from nearly 50 per cent in 1955 to less than 36 per cent in October 1974. In the words of one commentator, the results of the two general elections in 1974 were 'warning shots' to the main parties that they could no longer take for granted their claim to monopolise British government. Several MPs, previously Labour, the most notable of whom was Dick Taverne, stood as Independents in 1974 and won, though only once.

In 1979, although the election result was once more a decisive one, the detailed figures revealed that the underlying trend was the same. In spite of the fact that the share of the popular vote going to the two main parties rose to 80 per cent, and the Conservatives won a clear majority of forty-three seats, the fragmentation of the party system remained evident. The election campaign had had 'much of the character of an unpopularity contest' (Bogdanor 1981, p. 173). There was no united national verdict. There were twenty-seven MPs in the House who did not owe allegiance to either major party, indeed minor parties had gained 18 per cent of the votes, and although Liberals and Nationalists fell back from their pre-election position, they were not entirely unsuccessful, with eleven Liberal seats and four Nationalist ones. In addition, regional variations in the 'swing' left whole areas in which one of the major parties was more or less unrepresented. Labour lacked any representation in agricultural seats in England, and in large areas of the south and south-west. The Conservatives remained weak in the North and in the major cities, except London. The centrifugal tendencies of the system were very clear.

The decline in support for the Conservative and Labour parties was in part due to abstentions, but it was also the result of the gradual growth of a multi-party system. Between 1965 and 1975 the two-and-a-bit system had been replaced by one with seven parties; in addition to Conservative, Labour and Liberal there were the two nationalist parties and two Irish parties. With the partial exception of the Liberals, who remain to some extent on the 'Celtic fringe', these minor parties are entirely regional parties. Although in England an increasing number of seats are won on a minority vote, (see McKie, Cook and Phillips, 1979, pp. 190–91), this was really a Scottish, Welsh and Irish phenomenon. In October 1974 an amazing 43.6 per cent of all votes cast in those three countries were cast for minor parties. Major parties no longer sought votes in Northern Ireland; indeed all the parties active there were exclusively Irish. Small wonder that political commentators began to write about the break-up of the United Kingdom.

It was on the same issue of devolution during the 1974–9 Parliament that some of the changes discussed above made their impact on Parliament. Numerous deals were made by the Callaghan government, but it was on the issue of devolving some power to Scottish and Welsh assemblies that the government had to give most ground and which finally brought it down. Had it not been for the threat posed by the nationalist parties, the proposals – which had originally been mooted at the end of the 1960s at the time of the first nationalist by-election successes – might not have been revived. For the beleaguered Labour government, the proposals became a means of obtaining nationalist support; the first bill was introduced at the end of 1976. The government subsequently gave in to demands that the Scottish and Welsh people should be consulted in a referendum, but the bill was killed by opposition to the guillotine by a combination of Conservatives, Liberals and Labour back-benchers. New bills – one each for Scotland and Wales – were introduced in July 1977, by which time the government had secured the support of the Liberals. But these were amended by back-benchers so that they could not pass into law unless the referendum showed a 40 per cent vote in their favour.

Although the Lib–Lab pact – itself as much of a departure in British constitutional practice as devolution or the referendum – kept the government in office for far longer than would otherwise have been possible, its final defeat was the result of the failure of either of the two referenda to endorse the devolution proposals. The government had now lost the support of both Liberals and Scottish Nationalists. The crucial vote was lost by a margin of only one: a situation which could have been reversed if Reginald Prentice had not joined the Conservative Party eighteen months earlier. Thus James Callaghan became the first Prime Minister since Ramsay MacDonald in 1924 to suffer this kind of defeat.

Although the 1979 election brought the Conservatives into office with a firm majority, and the tradition of strong government was once more re-asserted, politics seemed more polarised than ever. The two-party system was dealt a further heavy blow by the success of the new Social Democratic Party. Not only does the SDP now constitute a far larger block in the House than any of the minor parties have previously done, but opinion polls at times indicated strong support in the electorate. This support comes as much from former Conservative as from former Labour voters. And the Party's electoral alliance with the Liberals could make it a formidable challenger to the two old parties accustomed to take turns at governing; in these circumstances the first-past-the-post electoral system may well come to be seen more widely as distorting the views and wishes of the electorate.

At the time of writing, only two of the new party's MPs, Roy Jenkins and Shirley Williams, had been elected on the party's ticket. The others, numbering more than twenty, were with the exception of one Conservative, formerly Labour Members. Many of these had faced dificulties in their constituencies, either in the reselection process, or as a result of boundary changes. Though it is not part of the task of this book to give an account of how the new party came to be founded, the developments in the Labour Party since 1970, and in particular the campaign for reselection of MPs, which are its main concerns, are in a sense the other side of the same coin. For reselection was an important contributing factor to the foundation of the new party. But before considering the question of selection and reselection, it is necessary first to discuss how the British constitution has traditionally seen the role of the Member of Parliament.

2   The role of the representative – an historical introduction

In 1972 the Tribune Group of Labour MPs published a pamphlet (Allaun, Mikardo and Sillars, 1972) which set out to make the case for greater democracy in the Labour party. It included the following remarks:

> It is time Burke was put in his place – Burke himself was no democrat and since he spoke a new world has been born. We do not live in Burke's world any more, and it is time the Parliamentary Party understood that the aristocratic concepts which ruled these islands in the eighteenth century are unfitted for a modern democracy.

But representation and in particular the role of the Member of Parliament is often discussed in terms redolent of past centuries, with only a veneer of modernity. The extension of the vote to all and universal education has changed the political system in a basic way.[1] In spite of this, the Whig view of representation, and in particular Burke's formulation of the proper role of a representative, has been remarkably durable. At the same time, it has been perennially controversial and has frequently been argued afresh when disputes have arisen between MPs and their constituency parties. This study will concern itself chiefly with such cases, the marginal ones, in an attempt to throw light on the dilemmas that face Members of Parliament in contemporary Britain. But if we are to understand the separate layers of theory which inform the debate on representation, we must first return to Burke.

Burke's speech to the electors of Bristol, made in 1774, is the major source for his views, and it is, therefore, worth quoting from it at length.

> . . . it ought to be the happiness and glory of a representative to live in the strictest union, the closest correspondence, and the most un-

[1] 'The formalisms of the British Constitution are expressive of a society in which authority was seen to flow easily and unquestioningly from governments and political leaders. But a society in which authority resides in the electorate, and legitimacy is conferred primarily by popular election, can function successfully only if it adapts itself to the consequences, however delayed, of universal suffrage and the spread of education.' (Bogdanor, 1981, p. 4.)

reserved communication with his constituents. Their wishes ought to have great weight with him; their opinions high respect; their business unremitted attention. It is his duty to sacrifice his repose, his pleasure, his satisfactions to theirs, – and above all, ever, and in all cases, to prefer their interest to his own.

But his unbiased opinion, his mature judgement, his enlightened conscience, he ought not to sacrifice to you – your representative owes you, not his industry only, but his judgement: and he betrays, instead of serving you, if he sacrifices it to your opinion.

My worthy colleague says, his will ought to be subservient to yours. If that be all, the thing is innocent. If Government were a matter of will upon any side, yours, without question, ought to be superior. But Government and legislation are matters of reason and judgement, and not of inclination; and what sort of reason is that in which the determination precedes the discussion, in which one set of men deliberate and another decide, and where those who form the conclusion are perhaps three hundred miles distant from those who hear the arguments?

To deliver an opinion is the right of all men; that of constituents is a weighty and respectable opinion, which a representative ought always to rejoice to hear, and which he ought always most seriously to consider. But *authoritative* instructions, *mandates* issued, which the member is bound blindly and implicitly to obey, to vote, and to argue for, though contrary to the clearest conviction of his judgement and conscience, – these are things utterly unknown to the laws of this land, and which arise from a fundamental mistake of the whole order and tenor of our constitution.

Parliament is not a *congress* of ambassadors from different and hostile interests – but Parliament is a *deliberative* assembly of *one* nation, with *one* interest, that of the whole – where not local purpose, not local prejudices ought to guide, but the general good, resulting from the general reason of the whole. You choose a member indeed; but when you have chosen him, he is not a member of Bristol, but he is a member of Parliament. (Speech to the electors of Bristol, 1774; reprinted in Hill 1975, pp. 156 ff.).

This became, in the nineteenth century, the accepted definition of the relation between an MP and his constituents, one of the few elements in the unwritten constitution which dated back to the eighteenth century. It was accepted also in other European states, post-revolutionary France among them (Birch, 1972, pp. 46–8).

The famous speech, however, was not looking to the future, but was made for a precise political purpose, and in a particular historical context: 'The country was knocking at the door of Parliament and demanding electoral reform' (Butt 1967, p. 57). As Eulau and his colleagues (1959) point out, later theorists have ignored Burke's 'contextual basis and polemical bias'. Relying as he usually did, on historical precedent, Burke argued that mandates and instructions were unknown to the laws of the land; this was intended as a warning to the electors of Bristol, who were known to hold radical views on the subject. The other MP elected with him shared their views, and Burke was anxious that he might be forced to campaign for radical reform, which was already being demanded, and which he strongly opposed (Hill, 1975, p. 156).

In addition to reacting against the radical movement, 'it does no harm to recall that there was a still older view in light of which Burke's idea was subversive' (Beer, 1957, p. 615). This view, promulgated by Bolingbroke among others (see Birch, 1964, p. 27 and Kramnick in Pennock and Chapman (eds.), 1975, p. 87), saw the King as being the representative of the national interest, and MPs as the delegates of their constituents, their chief function being to grant supply of funds to the King (Beer, 1965, pp. 614-5), but also being occupied with local and special interest. The Whig view, which later came to predominate, gave the members of the House of Commons a special role as *national* representatives, but Burke's precise political interest at the time was to assert the importance of the elected representatives against what he saw as the excessive influence of the Crown in the 1760s and 1770s. Not that he opposed the influence of the monarchy; rather the reverse, he saw it as part of the balanced constitution and merely wanted to do away with abuses and excesses, in particular the influence of the 'court party'. This aim was also the source of his support for the idea of parties and of a concerted opposition, anathema to the Tories. However, although Burke favoured the concept that MPs should be national representatives and that the chief function of the House should be deliberative, government at the time was chiefly by administration. Legislation was not of major importance. Thus the trusteeship advocated by Burke was of a defensive nature: 'thus members of parliament don't rule; they defend the people against royal misrule' (Conniff, 1977, p. 340). Nor, in spite of his spirited defence of party, did Burke see the deliberations of the House as culminating in divisions, but rather the emergence of a consensus.

Although Burke's brilliant language and persuasive argument have contributed to the durability of his thought, the views he propounded were not new; Walpole was a major source for his thinking on the independence of the representative. He had written forty years before:

> ... we have no right to send threatening letters and insolent instructions, authorisation orders and commands to those persons in whom we have lodged the supreme power of legislation. (*London Journal*, 1734, quoted by Kramnick in Pennock and Chapman (eds.). 1975).

The idea that MPs once elected should use their own judgement rather than act as delegates of their constituents was also stated in the writings of

Algernon Sidney; in *Discourses Concerning Government*, published in 1698, he wrote:

> It is not [therefore] for Kent or Sussex, Lewes or Maidstone, but for the whole nation, that members chosen to serve in these places are sent to serve in Parliament. And though it be fit for them to hearken to the opinions of the electors for the information of their judgements, and to the end that what they say may be of more weight...yet they are not strictly and properly obliged to give account of their actions to any, unless the whole body of the nation for which they serve, and who are equally concerned in their resolutions, could be assembled. This being impracticable, the only punishment to which they are subject, if they betray their trust, is scorn, infamy, hatred, and an assurance of being rejected when they shall again seek the same honour (quoted in Birch, 1964, p. 29).

Although the passage of the 1832 Reform Act swept away most of the Whig theory of representation, Burke's formulation of the MP/constituency relation remained supported by the rules of parliamentary privilege, to become one strand in the Liberal theory which replaced it. But already by then significant changes had taken place in the political system and in the wider context of English life. These have only become more marked with the passage of time, and present problems for Burke's formula; there are several aspects of this which will be dealt with in turn.

First, Burke was very far from being a democrat, even in a limited sense. The main purpose of many of his writings and speeches, as Macpherson (1980) has so compellingly argued, was to defend an established hierarchical society. All his presumptions were in favour of old institutions: 'It is a presumption in favour of any settled scheme of government against any untried project, that a nation has long existed and flourished under it' (quoted in Macpherson, 1980, p. 41). His opposition to electoral reform was based on this:

> It [the British Constitution] is a constitution, whose sole authority is that it has existed time out of mind (quoted in Macpherson, 1980, p. 40).

He was vehemently opposed to majority rule; indeed he thought that property should be disproportionately represented in order to protect it adequately (Macpherson, 1980, p. 47), and even doubted that the individual had any political rights at all.

> As to the share of power, authority and direction which each individual ought to have in the management of the state, that I must deny to be amongst the direct original rights of man in civil society... (quoted in Macpherson, 1980, p. 43).

All of these views, perfectly acceptable in their own time, are so out of tune with current thinking that they might indeed rule Burke 'out of court for the late twentieth century', (Macpherson, 1980, p. 74). Certainly they reduce his appeal to those seeking to improve democratic processes. What is missing in the quotations above is any democratic impulse in the sense of any concept of responsiveness or accountability. It is unacceptable to democratic thought today that the interests of the electorate should be decided entirely by others; it is necessary for the representative to be responsive to the wishes of his constituents. This view had much greater influence later on, under the impact of nineteenth century individualism, and many interpretations of Burke have depicted him as denying that the representative should be accountable at all. An American scholar and student of Burke has attacked these interpretations as inaccurate, arguing that Burke did indeed believe in accountability (Conniff, 1977).

Burke, according to this view, believed that in order successfully to counterbalance the power of the monarchy, Parliament must be close to the people.

> The closer the relationship between the people and their represent-atives, the better able those representatives will be to stand against the persuasions of the ministers and the greater the opportunity of the constituents to notice any lapse in the zeal of their members. (Burke, quoted in Conniff, 1977, p. 335.)

The people then are to express their grievances, and the representatives are to seek the remedy, with as much freedom of action as possible. Burke believed in popular control, within the limits of the existing franchise:

> The people are the masters – they are the sufferers, they tell the symptoms of the complaint; but we know the exact seat of the disease and how to apply the remedy. (Burke, quoted in Conniff, 1977, p. 336.)

Thus although Burke demanded independence, this was not a complete independence, and he very clearly defended the right of the electors to dismiss him. Indeed, six years after the famous speech, in 1780, he stood down at the request of his Bristol constituents, having been at odds with them for most of that time on the question of the American war and the anti-Catholic laws (Conniff, 1977, p. 332). He admitted that he had not visited the city, and on the disputed issues defended himself with the assertion that he was better informed than they were, and that his views were right. But they had every right to dismiss him:

> . . . I received your trust in the face of day, and in the face of day I accept your dismission.

The ultimate sanction, then, was the electorate's and the representative is accountable to them.

In recent years, several MPs in dispute with their constituency parties have used Burke's phrases as indicating their right to take their dispute to a wider forum than that provided by the party. This is not a necessary conclusion. Burke spoke when there was no properly established party system. He argued that those who elected him had every right to ask him to stand down, for any reason at all (Conniff, 1977, p. 339). But they were only a few in number, and there was no party organisation, local or national, to interpose itself between the candidates and the electors.

In Burke's day, the franchise was extremely restricted. He calculated 'the people' to number approximately 400,000 – less then the population of present-day Bristol. There were already, as we have seen, demands for radical reform, and indeed the demand for manhood suffrage had been heard as long ago as the 1640s, in the days of the Levellers. The rise of Benthamite utilitarianism in the nineteenth century, with its emphasis on the individual and on the representation of opinions rather than interests led not only to the passing of the 1832 Reform Act, the first major change, but also as Birch (1964, p. 52) says, opened the gates to 'further instalments of reform'. Representation was henceforth to be by population, thus doing away with the Whig principle of virtual representation; universal suffrage, though still a long way off, was the logical implication. The Whig theory was thus gradually replaced by the Liberal one, crudely summed up in the phrase 'one man, one vote, one value'.[1]

The second change that transformed the eighteenth century political system was the development of the mass party. This was largely the result of the passing of a second Reform Act in 1867, which almost doubled the electorate. The number of voters was by then so large that the parties in Parliament, now well-established, found it necessary to extend their operations more systematically into the country in order to influence the new voters.

Although Burke has been described as the 'philosopher of party', he did not by any means anticipate this development. By party he had meant small groups acting together within the Commons, not the coherent parliamentary parties observed later by Bagehot, still less the mass political organisations which had become a vital part of the system by the end of the nineteenth century. In the years that followed the 1832 Reform Act, the party system as we know it today was established (see Butt, 1967, Chapter 2); and the idea of an MP being independent was already under strain, even in the rather chaotic parliamentary conditions which followed the repeal of the Corn Laws. Two remarks from eminent parliamentary leaders are worth quoting. Disraeli, criticising a Government which had

---

[1] But the issue of legislative apportionment has never been as controversial here as it has in the USA.

had to abandon most of its legislation for lack of a majority, said:

> You cannot choose between Party government and parliamentary government. I say, you can have no parliamentary government if you have no party government (quoted in Butt, 1967, p. 73).

The need for strong party discipline was also supported by Salisbury, who wrote:

> The independent-member theory – the notion of 635 men, each studying every question for himself, and voting on his own judgement of its merits without bias or favour – is an inspiration from Laputa[1]... Combinations there must be (quoted in Butt, 1967, p. 72).

In the second half of the nineteenth century party allegiances were tightened. Liberals and Conservatives dominated the House under the leadership of Gladstone and Disraeli. The party leaders had a direct relationship with the electorate; policy was increasingly floated in the country, and Disraeli resigned after his defeat in the 1868 election without even meeting the House. Candidates increasingly depended on the new party organisations, which were improved after the election defeats for the Conservatives in 1868 and the Liberals in 1874; in addition, improved communications made relations between MPs and their local parties closer than they had ever been.

Fears that the new situation would threaten the independence of MPs were widely expressed; Ostrogorski's critique was probably the most eloquent. His fears, as shown in Chapter 1, focused on the caucus, or extra-parliamentary organisation. Although it had facilitated government by supplying majorities, he argued, it had also 'warped the representative principle on which parliamentary government reposes', and which consists in the 'personal confidence with which the Member inspires the electors, who trust him to manage the affairs of the nation on their behalf'. The caucus, he went on, 'tended to eliminate, or at any rate to diminish, the personal element in the relations between the Member and his constituents'. Once returned, party orthodoxy is forced on the MP: 'Unable to use his discretion freely, and prevented from seeking his political line of conduct in his own knowledge and conscience, the Member ceases to be a representative' (Ostrogorski, 1964, pp. 313–4). Ostrogorski himself immediately admits, however, that universal suffrage itself would have the same effect: 'The regime of a widely extended suffrage, however, is moving in this direction of itself; when the number of voters becomes too great to allow of personal contact, from which the Member derives his

---

[1]Laputa: from Swift's satire *Gulliver's Travels*; 'In Laputa, Gulliver finds the wise men so wrapped up in their speculations as to be utter dotards in practical affairs' (Oxford Companion to English Literature, 4th edn. p. 359).

inspiration direct, and the electors their trust in his judgement, relations of confidence necessarily give way to formal pledges.'

The development of the mass party strengthened the position of the party leadership. But the procedural reforms introduced in the Commons in the 1880s also considerably restricted the opportunities for back-benchers; these were introduced by Gladstone as a check on the obstruct-ion persistently practised by Irish MPs, and they included restricting the use of adjournment motions and the introduction of the closure and the guillotine. Together these changes represented 'the watershed between the old and the new government-managed Parliament' (Butt, 1967, p. 88). The power of parliamentary leaders was thus greatly enhanced, both in the House and in the country. Elections became a personal contest between Gladstone and Disraeli, who were able to use the mass media of their times, the popular press, to appeal directly to the people, who no longer needed the MP 'to shape their views by' (Ostrogorski, 1964, p. 318). The local caucus was a weapon in the hands of the leadership to control any recalcitrant members.

The effects of these developments were only strengthened by the further extension of the franchise; the government gradually took over the time of the House, starting in the nineteenth century, and culminating in the Balfour reforms of 1902 and those under Attlee in 1945. Only in this way could the House deal with the mass of new legislation demanded by the newly enfranchised from the 1830s on; after the doubling of the electorate by the 1918 Representation of the People Act and the advent of the first working-class MPs, the party organisations were in general the only means of getting and keeping a seat in Parliament and: 'The new political status of Labour at Westminster was an important influence in changing the relationship of the political parties represented in Parliament with the electorate' (Butt, 1967, p. 99).

Labour's gradual rise to the position of the main opposition party further increased both the importance of party organisation and of party discipline; 'the idea of the independent MP was squeezed to the bone' (Butt, 1967, p. 105). Labour's view of representation strongly favoured the delegate view: and the fears that this evokes have recurred inter-mittently to the present day. But it is clear that the political system had undergone a fundamental change. While its tasks in a general sense remain the same – the provision of government and the reconciliation of conflict, for instance – the universal franchise alters the way in which the system is viewed. This difference has been given controversial expression by Macpherson. He points out that Burke's task was to 'persuade the ruling-class to resist any ideas which would weaken the still prevailing working-class acceptance of the established hierarchical order'. In contrast, the task that faces contemporary liberals, he says, is to 'legitimate the presently established modified capitalist order, or some variant of it, in the eyes of a somewhat politically conscious and quite strongly organised western working-class' (Macpherson, 1980, p. 73). One does not need to share Macpherson's view of the state as an instrument of class to agree that legitimacy is a more pressing issue once everyone has the vote and thus in theory equal political rights.

In addition, the environment in which the political system has to operate is greatly altered; not only are there mass party organisations, but a vast expansion of government activity and the development of all kinds of pressure groups which are in effect instruments of functional representation *outside* Parliament and the party system. At the same time, the issues of modern politics are infinitely more complex than those of Burke's day. In response to these changes, other writers have developed a variety of theories of representation: one of these, which originates from Bentham, has had a powerful influence on the debate. This 'microcosmic' or 'descriptive' view of representation, which holds that a representative should share some of the characteristics or qualities of those he represents, is often appealed to in political and nonpolitical contexts. Lord Boothby once said: 'Ideally, the House of Commons should be a social microcosm of the nation. The nation includes a great many people who are rather stupid, and so should the House' (quoted in Birch, 1972, pp. 58–9). But there is no valid reason to think that a representative will serve his constituents better because he resembles them; as it has been argued, we should not allow lunatics to be represented by lunatics (Phillips Griffiths, 1960).

This brief mention of descriptive representation serves to show up some of the paradoxes involved in the concept of representation. The oldest and most obvious of these is the delegate–trustee dichotomy; should the representative be the delegate of his constituents, carrying out their instructions, or an independent trustee who uses his own judgement? Either extreme can easily be shown to be unworkable; the question is at what point on the continuum between delegate and trustee is most acceptable and most conducive to fulfilling the various functions of representation.

The delegate view has generally been one of outsiders, with the exception of some early American writers, who followed similar lines to Tom Paine and Robespierre. The authors of the *Federalist* papers thought that representatives should promote sectional interests, and favoured frequent elections to ensure 'dependence on, and an intimate sympathy with the people' (Birch, 1972, p. 42). Unlike English thinkers, they believed in popular sovereignty, but the Americans also had a counterweight to this in the separation of powers, and an indirectly elected President.

This system can, however, pose a threat if there is a deep division within society, as Calhoun saw. Writing more than fifty years later and foreseeing secession if not the civil war, he doubted the optimism of Madison and his colleagues, and feared majority rule by the more powerful, anti-slave North. His 'concurrent majority' principle would have protected the Southern minority. Calhoun's views are relevant not only to American history and political thought, but to all discussions of representative government, because they show up the limitations of delegated represent-ation: disagreements can only be solved so long as they are open to com-promise (Birch, 1972, p. 86). 'If politics is more than a matter of balancing group pressures the elected representative, in so far as he is a policy maker, must act as rather more than a delegate' (Birch, 1972, p. 88).

Also at the heart of this controversy is the question of the relative cap-abilities of the representative and the constituents. Closely related is the issue of whether the representative should promote the desires or wishes of his constituents, as opposed to their welfare or interests. Does the ignorance of the majority, as J. S. Mill maintained, render their judgement unreliable and their opinions of doubtful value? Those who follow an extreme independent line would argue that political questions are beyond ordinary people, and that political judgements should, therefore, be made by their representatives. Burke's chief defence against the electors of Bristol on the disputed issues was that he knew better than they did. J. S. Mill, following Burke, stressed the necessity of choosing superior minds as representatives (1972, p. 317).[1] They, he argued, were more likely to be right if a difference of opinion occurred; but while emphasising the importance of deferring to mental superiority, he found it difficult to lay down hard-and-fast rules on the matter, which he saw as a question of the ethics of representative government. The electors could make the MP their delegate if they so wished, but they would be unwise to insist on absolute conformity with their opinions in view of his superior know-ledge. On the other hand, he detected a strand of opinion which tended to defer to the constituents:

> ... there is a floating notion of the opposite kind, which has consider-able practical operation on many minds, even of members of Parlia-ment, and often makes them, independently of desire for popularity, or concern for their re-election, feel bound in conscience to let their conduct, on questions on which their constituents have a decided opinion, be the expression of that opinion rather than their own (p. 315).

These generalisations, however, fail to cope with the complications which may arise for the delegate position. What if the constituents have no wishes, or indeed if a diverse constituency includes a wider range of

[1]Mill, like Burke, gave a high priority to preserving property, and his scheme included a provision for plural voting, a major qualification to his theory of representation, indeed an attempt to rig the system.

opinion on a particular issue? Thus the inherent weakness of the delegate theory rests on the remote probability of a single, clear expression of opinion arising. In these circumstances, it is argued, the representative will in effect be forced to move closer to the trustee position, and develop a view of his own, which would probably be an amalgam of personal and party views plus a view of what would be best for the constituents.

Eulau and his colleagues (1959) distinguish three 'role orientations' which an elected representative may adopt: Delegate, Trustee, and in the intermediate position, Politico. In the case of Delegates, the possibility of conflict is clearly envisaged, and decided in favour of subordination to the represented. Trustees tend to place a higher priority on moral values, but are also likely to say that their constituents had little information or did not know what they wanted. Politicos are generally more flexible and less dogmatic. The conclusion of the study is that in contemporary society, ordinary people frequently cannot understand the problems of government, so representatives are likely to become 'trustees' more and more.

The delegate/trustee issue has become confused with another issue, that of whether the representative is to further the interests of his local district or of the whole nation. Ernest Barker saw it as a single issue in his writings on Burke. He contrasts 'a free and national representative' to 'an attentive member of a local constituency ... acknowledging a prior loyalty to its opinions and interests'. As Burke put it: 'You choose a Member indeed; but when you have chosen him, he is not a member of Bristol, but he is a member of Parliament.' (Quoted in Barker, 1951, p. 182.) This is, Eulau *et al* point out, to confuse focus with style: the fact that a representative sees himself as following his own judgement does not mean that he is necessarily likely to promote a general rather than a particular interest (1959, p. 745). Although distinguishing between the two, the Eulau study sees that they are related to one another. Their study of legislators in four US states revealed that those whose orientation was to the whole state – and therefore, had no state-wide clientele to which to refer – were more likely to be Trustees than Delegates, while those who were district-orientated were more likely to be Delegates. The issues, while distinct, are linked in a 'system of mutually interpenetrating orientations'.

David Judge puts an interesting gloss on this widely accepted analysis: what appears to be important in determining the style of representation is not the focus but the *homogeneity* of interest or opinion encompassed within the focus (Judge, 1981, p. 34). The delegate style of representation, he argues, is both analytically and empirically linked with a specific focus of representation. A purely delegate style, he suggests, can only be possible for a cohesive and coherent *functional* constituency, not a territorial one. If the interests of the functional group are well-known and agreed, and there is frequent consultation, a delegate style can probably work well. Judge points out nicely the distinction between an electorate in which interests and opinions are heterogeneous, not easily identifiable, where unforeseen contingencies arise and one which has homogeneous, readily identifiable interests and is in constant contact with its representative.

It was this sort of constituency that was envisaged by G.D.H. Cole in his various writings on Guild Socialism though his position on the delegate–trustee issue was by no means consistent. For Cole, however, true representation had to be functional and specific. Guild Socialist ideas, which were collectivist in their inspiration, and thus in conflict with the liberal theory of parliamentary institutions which was about the representation of individuals, was only one of several successive waves of alternative views on representation which made their influence felt during the nineteenth and twentieth centuries. The result is confusion about the proper role of a representative. The Liberal theory of the constitution has been eroded by the influence of these ideas – Idealist, Syndicalist, Guild Socialist, Socialist, etc. – and by the enormously enlarged task which is faced by governments today compared with those in the nineteenth century.

But the Burkean view of an MP's role was still widely held in spite of the fact that it was difficult to reconcile with party government. The dislike of Whigs, Tories and Liberals for organised political parties was, as we have mentioned, gradually eroded in the nineteenth century. Party gradually came to be seen 'not as violating independence but positively enhancing it by attaching individuals to steady and lasting principles' (Beer, 1965, p. 39). However, when the Labour Representation Committee was founded in 1900 its object was specifically to ensure the representation in Parliament of the working class as *a group*. By deciding that its candidates should be chosen only from groups associated with the ILP, the trade unions or the Cooperative Movement, and by defining its aims only in terms of working-class interest, the party was, it can be argued (Birch, 1964, p. 88), rejecting the Liberal theory of representation in favour of a collectivist theory.

The party was interposed between individuals and their representatives, and the idea of a mandate meant that an MP was a delegate, but not necessarily a local one (Beer, 1965, p. 87). Herein lies the perennial controversy in the Labour party over the role of its MP *vis-à-vis* the Annual Conference and the other extra parliamentary organs of the party.

The structure of the party, with the conference as the supreme policy-making body, to which the parliamentary party was theoretically subject, not only held the seeds of future conflict, but might also be seen as a denial of the sovereignty of Parliament. In practice, however, the parliamentary leadership retained control of policy-making most of the time, and Labour

MPs at least, remained committed to the traditional principles of parliamentary government. Socialism by parliamentary methods was justified by what Birch has called the 'theory of the mandate' or 'manifestoism'.

> The party nominates parliamentary candidates; these candidates commit themselves, if elected to Parliament, to 'carry out the provisions of the manifesto'; a manifesto is written for each election by the NEC; it is the collective duty of Labour's representatives to criticise Government actions on the basis of the manifesto when Labour is out of office and to enact it when it is in office. (Drucker, 1979, p. 92.)

This, Drucker argues, is an ideology rather than a theory; and an ideology which is primarily about representation, and only indirectly about government (1979, p. 92). But it has been adopted by other parties, not only in the United Kingdom, as a theory of government or a justification of a government's conduct. However, as this, or as a theory of representation, it has faults. It makes no allowances for the government's need to adjust to changing circumstances; or for the fact that the party's conference delegates may not see the world as it really is. What is more, manifestoes are 'occasionally contradictory, frequently vague and rarely put in any order of priority' (1979, p. 92).[1]

The party's constitution itself is vague on which organs of the party have responsibility in different matters; especially relevant to this discussion is the confusion over the position of the party's MPs.

> Is an MP responsible to the National Executive Committee, who are charged with interpreting the resolutions of the Annual Conference and writing the manifesto; or is he responsible to his constituency party, who in fact selected him as the party's candidate and who can decide whether or not to re-adopt him; or to the Annual Conference; or to the party whip who can deny him preferment; or is he responsible to some combination of these groups? (Drucker, 1979, p. 93.)

It has been argued in a more general context (Pennock and Chapman (eds.), 1968, Chapter 1), that as government functions expand, the tensions of party discipline for the individual representative will increase if he is expected to support the party's programme in all its aspects. Labour MPs are in theory committed to this; and MPs of other parties can also find themselves in a difficult position. It becomes less and less likely, it can be argued, that the party will arrive at a programme with which most of its members agree; in the future parties might become less programmatic and less disciplined.

---

[1] In addition, recent studies have clearly shown that voters do not vote on the basis of what is in the manifestoes of the parties.

Certainly, the pressures on some MPs during the Labour Government of 1964–70 were such that party discipline was relaxed. It has been suggested that 'it may not be possible for rigid discipline to be exerted over the PLP when the Conference and the Party leaders have deeply conflicting policy perspectives' (Minkin, 1978b, p. 310).[1] This has also been true of the Conservative Party during Mrs Thatcher's Government. The pressures on contemporary MPs are thus seen to be far removed in many ways from those that faced Burke.

Three separate strands of thought – Burkean, Liberal and Collectivist – all play a part in current thinking on representation (see Judge, 1981, p. 41). Burkean theory, although denied by current political practice, is still alive. It is still powerful in the procedural rules of the House, and in some sections of the electorate; it was invoked in some of the conflicts which we shall look at in the ensuing chapters, and is seen as an *éminence grise* by the Labour Left, as the quotation at the beginning of this chapter showed, Simultaneously, many MPs and voters subscribe to the mandate theory too. Thus the common view of the MP's proper role is an amalgam of different theories; for the representative, at least, these serve to provide a strong bond between the MP and his constituents. This bond is inevitably subject to tension. There is always a potential for conflict, but conflict should not customarily occur: 'The representative must act in such a way that there is no conflict, or if it occurs an explanation is called for. He must not be found persistently at odds with the wishes of the represented.' (Pitkin, 1967, p. 209). The relationship between the MP and his constituency will be examined more closely in Chapter 3.

---

[1]But a revision of the code of conduct for the PLP in 1968 ruled out changes which would have protected dissident MPs if they were voting in accordance with Conference decisions.

3   The MP and his constituency

The historical events and the developments in theoretical thinking that have influenced views about the role of an MP were examined in Chapter 2. MPs have a dual responsibility, being both national representatives at Westminster and representatives of the constituency. The primary role of the MP is at Westminster, where MPs collectively are traditionally held to represent the nation. 'The sense of the nation', Nigel Nicolson wrote, 'will only emerge if the individual Member considers his national responsibility to be even greater than his constituency one' (Nicolson, 1958, p. 172). Written only in 1958, these words already have a curiously old-fashioned ring, an indication perhaps of the extent of the changes that have taken place in the political system in the last two decades. But whatever the changes, the greater part of the work of a Member of Parliament remains *in* Parliament, supporting the Government or opposing it, perhaps on the front benches, discussing national and international affairs in the Chamber, or involved in committee work, scrutinising legislation or the work of the executive branch. At Westminster particularly, he is a party man. As Chapter 2 described, the development of political parties in the nineteenth century, though feared at first, was later welcomed as offering Members a coherent set of principles to which they could attach themselves.

In spite of the fact that the business of the House is under the control of the main parties, most MPs feel that they can in some aspects of their work remain independent representatives. They may manifest this independence by specialising in particular areas of national policy, or supporting particular causes. However, for most MPs, it is in their work as constituency representatives that they can most readily assert their individual judgement and influence. It is with the role of the MP within his constituency that this chapter is concerned.

Examining the MP's role as a constituency representative raises all the vexed questions discussed in Chapter 2: whether an MP should act as a delegate or as a trustee, whether his preoccupations should be primarily local or national, as well as whether he should follow the party line or reflect the view of a majority of his constituents. Before election, every

MP is selected by a local party committee; local party members work in the campaign to secure his election; but it is the wider electorate, voting in the election, who actually return him to Westminster. If an MP is to retain his seat in Parliament, he will need at least to retain the support of all these groups. And if he is to become known as a good constituency MP he must be seen to respond to a whole range of pressures which spring from the demands of these different groups.

The changes that have taken place in British politics in the post-war years make the MP's constituency role more important than it was in the past. Increasingly, major questions of public policy are decided away from Westminster, for example after consultation between the government and organised groups. The 'sense of the nation' is no longer exclusively to be found in Parliament. In addition, appeals directly to the electorate, either via the mass media or by means of referenda as well as the use of opinion polls, have reduced the traditional conception of the MP's role as representing the collective will of the nation. Simultaneously, the expansion of government, including the establishment of the welfare state, has resulted in authority, whether local or national, impinging increasingly on the lives of individual citizens, who consequently have grievances in need of redress, for which they turn to their MP. For all these reasons, Members may feel that their constituency responsibility is a more important part of their job than in the past.

Certainly, the electorate places a high priority on this aspect of an MP's work. Survey evidence suggests that ordinary voters see the MP as a local trouble-shooter. The Granada TV Survey of 1973 indicated that the public does not want its MPs to be either lobby fodder for the political parties, orators, or keen scrutinisers of legislation.

> For the ordinary voter, the ideal MP is a local resident who devotes his full time to the job of dealing with their personal problems, conscientiously attending local functions and meetings; who occasionally sallies forth to express his constituents' views in the national debate at Westminster. (Crewe and Spence, 1973, pp. 78–80.)

Other surveys have supported this finding; and similar views have been expressed by those concerned in local government. For example, during the 1979 general election campaign, the Lord Mayor of Sheffield attacked the city's six Members of Parliament for failing to make known to the government the views of the city council. 'I am sick and tired,' he said, 'of our MPs concentrating on parliamentary government at the expense of local government' (Sheffield *Morning Telegraph*, 28 March 1979).

An MP's constituency duties, apart from strictly party ones, while not formally defined, can be divided into two main groups. At the level of the individual voter, the MP is a 'powerful friend', an intermediary between the citizen and authority; he is, 'in a sense, a kind of minor and part-time ombudsman' (Dowse, 1963, p. 341). Most MPs hold surgeries from time to time to which constituents will come to him for help. The issues raised at the surgeries are much more likely to be administrative than political in nature; they concern housing, social security and income tax. At least half of them are matters within the jurisdiction of local rather than national government. Not surprisingly, this surgery work is not generally seen by MPs as being political, though it may gain them votes; but at the same time, MPs have no place in the central administrative structure, nor are they integrated in any way with the local institutions, though most MPs often have a councillor at surgeries with them. In fact relations with the local authority are quite frequently strained. The MP's position in the constituency remains an ambiguous one, and although some MPs see the redress of grievances as an 'essential link in democratic self-government' (Dowse, 1963, p. 341), it can also be argued that the need for this work indicates a failure of our system of administrative justice. Most studies of this aspect of an MP's work contain no feeling that this function could not have been carried out by someone else. One former MP concluded that 'a reasonably trained and sympathetic social worker could do most of this work adequately' (P. Rose, 1981, p. 90).

On the broader front, as well as seeking redress for individual grievances, the MP has a role as the 'official representative' of the constituency. He will speak for the district on its chief interest and problems; for instance, Eddie Milne saw it as his main task to speak up for the North East and its unemployment. Safeguarding the jobs of his constituents is likely to be a major preoccupation for any MP, but there are other issues of district-wide importance which concern him and his constituents, for instance transport problems in rural areas, agricultural policy, police/public relations, and many more. On all of these sorts of issues, the MP will speak for the whole electorate. He will also receive representations and requests for support from all kinds of local and national associations, pressure groups and trade unions. He may lend his name to a cause or raise a matter in the House, perhaps in association with other MPs. One MP recalls that 'sometimes I seemed to be no more than a receiver of deputations and go-between on local matters' (P. Rose, 1981).

This aspect of an MP's work may be seen as a link between the political activity in the country and the House of Commons, and it is less easy to imagine a substitute for it than for the surgery work. It is indeed a traditional parliamentary representative function:

> Elected representatives form conduits for the flood of the views of the electors and by their support enhance the effect of the flow. It is a proper Parliamentary role obviously clearly understood by those who communicate with their MP. (Morrell, 1977, p. 36.)

A good impression and a reasonable record of success in both of these areas are what adds up to being a 'good constituency MP'.

Constituency work may afford satisfaction to some MPs, although it is only partly seen as a vote-gathering exercise. The constituency connection keeps an MP's feet 'firmly on the ground' and enables him to keep in touch with local problems and 'take the political temperature' (P. Rose, 1981). In addition, it is possible for Members to find that Westminster is less enthralling than they had expected. There an MP may be 'mere lobby fodder, but in his constituency he is a VIP' (Mackintosh, 1978, p. 90). To some MPs, however, it is a heavy burden. Hard work in the constituency may limit an MP's ability to specialise, especially if he cannot afford paid assistance in the constituency to help with surgery and other work.

However, pleasing the broad constituency is not necessarily the same thing as satisfying the local party. It is they, or a few of their number, who selected the MP as a candidate and did the hard work of electioneering, and it is they who must re-nominate him before the next general election. Being a good constituency MP may go some way to satisfying the local party: Woodrow Wyatt found that 'Assiduity in performance as a welfare officer is a valuable aid to the MP in dealing with any difficulty he may have with his local party' (Wyatt, 1973, p. 85). But this is not always enough. Dick Taverne, during his dispute with the Lincoln Labour party, was widely stated to be a good constituency man, and he even quotes in support of this the findings of an opinion poll, which stated that 82 per cent of the electorate approved of his performance of his duties (Taverne, 1974, p. 76). In the disputes in East Aberdeenshire (1961) and Merthyr Tydfil (1970) local voters also declared themselves to be satisfied with their elected representative, although the local party wanted to dismiss him. Local party workers may take a different view from ordinary voters on what are the crucial issues of the day; in Lincoln, for example, local Labour activists felt very strongly about the Common Market issue, which was not an important one for the rest of the electorate.

What, then, do local party members want and expect from their MP? A detailed study of readoption disputes in both parties from 1948 to 1973 (Dickson, 1975) found that the satisfaction of the activists with the MP derives from four elements of an MP's role: his status with the parliamentary party, his contribution to constituency life, the establishment of 'satisfactory social ties within the constituency party' and his political beliefs as evidenced by statements and voting record in the House. Satisfactory performance in all four categories is not easily achieved.

Status in the parliamentary party is obviously important, but the effect of a front bench post may be the opposite of that expected; it may in fact alienate the local party. If an MP is a minister, he will have less time for the local duties which an MP is expected to fulfil. If the relationship with the local party is good, the minister may be forgiven for such omissions. Dick Taverne's view is that MPs do not enhance their position in the eyes of the local party by becoming ministers; it hinders their freedom of action on specific issues and prevents them from asking questions and from raising constituency matters on the floor of the House (Taverne, 1974, p. 37). They may also be too busy with ministerial duties to keep in proper contact with their local party. So, the prestige of having a minister for MP may please the local party, but equally its effects may not. There are a number of cases where a well-known national figure was replaced, on his retirement, by a local man. Two examples of this are Edward Boyle and Harold Lever, both of whom had had difficulties with their local parties. However, as the number of ministerial posts is limited, few MPs will in practice have this sort of trouble, but it does show that the local party members, as much as the uncommitted voters, want an MP who can relate to their problems rather than being wholly concerned with national issues.

Next, there is the MP's contribution to constituency life. What this means in practice is likely to be different in the Labour and Conservative parties. But because of the distance of the majority of constituencies from London, most MPs will only be weekend visitors. This is to be expected. Most of an MP's time is bound to be spent at Westminster and 'no MP can make himself the active centre of constituency affairs without pre-empting the responsibilities of constituency officers and neglecting his duties in the Commons' (R. Rose, 1976, p. 149). But the MP is expected to attend social functions, and some party meetings. His regular appearance is appreciated by party members and activists alike.

Thirdly, 'satisfactory social ties with the constituency party' are vital. No MP is dismissed by his local party if these particular relationships are soundly based, even though they are looked after on a part-time basis. Nor can a local party centre its activities exclusively around an MP who is present only for occasional weekends. Local elections are an equally important focus for the activists, even though the MP may not regard them as significant. Taverne found that his local officers were very pre-occupied with local and municipal elections, and that his own actions were often badly timed as far as these were concerned; he defied a three-line whip on the day of a local by-election and then resigned from the shadow cabinet during a municipal election campaign. Resentment from the local party officials was the result. The reverse may also be true; local issues may have an adverse effect on Westminster elections. Another Labour MP describes how his election to Parliament was overshadowed by local authority actions which might have affected the result to his disadvantage. (See Bryan Gould in Mackintosh, 1978, pp. 89–90).

Despite the inevitable difference of perspective, it is essential for the MP to keep on friendly terms with the local activists. Apparent arrogance on the part of the MP is especially unpopular. Taverne recalls that he should have spent more time drinking with the lads: 'I feel now in retrospect that I might have made a more determined effort to keep on good terms with people whose views I profoundly disagreed with' (1974, p. 76).

Lastly, the political beliefs of the MP are clearly important to his relationship with the constituency activists; this has been particularly true in the Labour Party in recent years. As noted earlier, David Butler, who had previously firmly held the view that 'divorce, drink or neglect of constituency business' were the cause of most readoption conflicts, now thinks that political reasons may play a larger part than they did in the past (Butler and Kavanagh, 1980, p. 280). The campaign within the Labour Party for reselection of MPs will be dealt with in detail later, but it is clear that in many constituency Labour parties today, the political views of the MP, including such questions as his attitude to the Common Market and to the left/right division in the party, especially as demonstrated by the recent battles over constitutional changes, are of the greatest importance for his relations with the constituency activists. Less active members of the party may take a more relaxed view; ideological considerations may be less important to them than years of service to the constituency and to the movement as a whole. But disputes over many years have also shown that personality conflicts are also an important factor. Where personal relationships are good, political disagreements may be tolerated. But where they are bad, and policy or ideology becomes a matter of conflict, all the conflicting demands of a representative's role become evident, and it is at this point that the party may seem to seek to dictate the actions of the MP, or alternatively try and dismiss him.

This is less frequently the case in the Conservative party. The lingering tradition of deference and the stronger hold which the Burkean ethos has over local Conservative associations mean that disputes of this kind, which have become almost commonplace in the Labour party, are rare. The Suez cases were exceptional, but showed that these problems are not unique to the Labour party. Suez and the difficulties that some MPs also encountered with their local associations as a result of voting in favour of capital punishment in a free vote led Robert McKenzie to comment:

> if the independently-minded Conservative MP now has little to fear from the Whips in Parliament, he may have a good deal to fear from the scorpions in the constituency associations (1963, p. 633).

On the whole, however, policy is not a major issue. The Conservative model rules for local associations make no mention of policy; indeed, Conservative Central Office warns local parties that they should not try to make their MP a spokesman for their own views.

The Labour Party, on the other hand, with its more complex power structure and greater ostensible commitment to democratic processes, has stood in theory at least, for rank-and-file participation in policy-making. The Labour Party sees itself as

> a collective expression of democratic sentiment based on the working class movement and on the constituency organisations of the workers (Quoted in McKenzie, 1963, p. 11).

In practice, until the 1970s constituency Labour parties had little or no influence either on the goals or the programme of the party nationally. And, as McKenzie argued, Labour was much like the Conservatives:

> once the candidate has been selected he need not thereafter undertake to conform to the views of his constituency party on any matter of policy.

Naturally there were limitations. Labour MPs could not consistently and with impunity ignore the views of local party members, any more than Conservative MPs could.

> Most Members of Parliament consider the views of their constituency party as one of a number of considerations, and by no means the most important one, to be taken into account when determining how they shall vote (McKenzie, 1963, p. 556).

As later chapters will show, Labour activists, disillusioned with the leadership and with its policies, have determined in recent years to increase their influence at local level by increasing pressure on the MP.

However, at this point the different views of MP, activists and the broader constituency may come into conflict. Not only may the MP and his local party officials be in disagreement on a particular major item of party policy, but the constituents as a whole may take the opposite view from that of the party activists. One example of this was a dispute between Woodrow Wyatt and his local Labour Party. During the 1964 Parliament, Wyatt was under attack from his local party activists for his opposition to the renationalisation of steel; he commissioned a market research survey – the first of its kind – to discover whether Labour voters in his Bosworth constituency agreed with his own views. The results suggested that they supported him. Armed with these results, Wyatt maintained his opposition to a major aspect of the government's programme. As a Labour MP, Wyatt was committed to the party manifesto which included as a prominent item the pledge to renationalise the steel industry. It was conference policy and was endorsed by a majority of the PLP. By all the tenets of the Labour Party, and it might be said of the Conservative Party as well, Wyatt was breaking ranks in a serious and divisive way by opposing the nationalisation proposals. His opposition, along with that of Desmond Donnelly, forced the government to abandon its bill.

Wyatt's justification for this action was that it was his obligation to represent the views of his constituency as a whole rather than the narrow interests of party activists. A similar kind of dilemma faced MPs of all parties on the Common Market question, and many followed Wyatt's example and conducted surveys or held referenda in their constituencies to ascertain the opinions of their constituents as a whole. The Common Market issue was exceptional. Not only was it a major departure in British policy, but it split both parties. In addition, the debate had been continuing for so long that most ordinary people might be expected to hold a view on the matter.

These difficulties which arise when the MP, the activists, and the electorate at large are in conflict with each other are not easily resolved. The average voter, even if he may want an MP who puts forward his own views rather than always following the party line, is not well informed, alert and attentive. In general MPs of all parties will not go against the party line except on issues in which they or their constituencies have a special interest, or of which they have special knowledge. It is only in such circumstances, or if the issue is of overwhelming importance to the country as a whole, that the MP begins to 'consider his duty as a Member of Parliament as well as a member of his party' (Nicolson, 1958, p. 71; see also, Dowse and Smith 1962–3). And MPs are unlikely to go to the lengths of consulting their electorates unless they are in clear disagreement with the local party leadership.

There is a remarkable similarity between the conflicts that Burke experienced as MP for Bristol from 1774 to 1780 and some more recent disputes. In spite of the passage of time, the issues raised then are almost identical to those that have confronted contemporary MPs. In 1780, when he had represented them for six years, there were four issues in the dispute between Burke and his constituents (see Barker, 1951, Chapter 4). The first was 'how much local residence, personal presence and social attendance' the constituency should expect. The rule that an MP should live in his constituency had only been abolished in 1774, though it had been in abeyance for many years. Burke had visited Bristol twice in six years, and admitted he had failed in this respect. 'An annual complimentary visit is a mark of decent attention and respect', he admitted.

The second issue was that of 'commissions' for local firms and individuals. Burke hated these, both because it distracted him from more important matters, but also because it drove him to dependence on the government. In his 1780 speech, he said:

I ran about wherever your affairs could call me, and in acting for you I often appeared rather as a shipbroker than as a Member of Parliament.

Thirdly was the well-worn issue of whether an MP should take instructions. On this, there 'had always been a contrast, we may almost say an incompatibility, between the man and his constituency'.

But there were also policy disagreements; Burke strongly opposed the American war and the anti-Catholic laws. His local electors did not hold the same views. Thus Burke had failed to make a sufficient contribution to constituency life, had not built up 'satisfactory social ties' with the electors, and they disagreed not only on several of the major issues of the day, but on the manner in which he should represent Bristol. His selection for the constituency had clearly been a mistake; it had been like 'a sudden love match, based on an ardent but ignorant affection, and divergencies of views and of temper began to appear as soon as the marriage was celebrated' (Barker, 1951, p. 202).

There is one significant difference. In Burke's time there were no central party organisations. Today, these play a part, albeit small, in candidate selection and in MP/constituency disputes. Their role has been well described by several writers. The central organisations act as a filter by providing lists of possible candidates and, in the case of the Labour Party, also have a veto power after selection.

In disputes between MPs and their local parties, action has varied but Labour Party Headquarters has generally been more active than its Conservative counterpart. In the late 1940s and 1950s, Transport House intervened a number of times in support of MPs whose left-wing management committees were reluctant to renominate them and four times expelled Labour MPs from the party. It also withheld endorsement from a number of candidates whose views were thought to be too left-wing; the recent cases of Peter Tatchell at Bermondsey and Pat Wall at Bradford North, whose candidatures the National Executive Committee has been reluctant to endorse, therefore represent more a return to past practice than a new departure.

When the Merthyr Tydfil Labour Party dismissed their MP S.O. Davies in 1970, the NEC definitely backed the party. And in the dispute between Muriel McKay and her local party in Clapham, party headquarters tried to defend her. The NEC in both cases was unsuccessful; indeed following the McKay dispute, the rules were changed to make the dismissal procedure less complex and allowed an appeal by the dismissed MP to the NEC. It was clear however, by 1972, that MPs in difficulties with their local parties would get no help from the leadership, the NEC or the party headquarters, and that any appeals were to be on procedural grounds only. This was partly a result of the Taverne affair, and of two long-standing disputes involving Neville Sandelson and Frank Tomney, but it also reflected the changed composition of the NEC, and the advent of the new party secretary, Ron Hayward.

Conservative Central Office has played a much less obtrusive role in disputes, though informal pressures are exerted, sometimes for, sometimes against the MP. In general, 'for the Conservative MP the first law of political survival is to cultivate and maintain the support of his association', as Harold Macmillan commented after the Nicolson case (Ranney, 1965, p. 87).

Some conflict between local and national organisations is seen as endemic in the system. The party headquarters takes a national view; it wants members, expertise and 'representativeness'. The local party inevitably takes a more parochial view; it wants the maximum poll, a member who will work well locally and remain in touch with his local party leadership.

The key relationship, then, is that between the MP and his local party. When disputes become serious, they are likely to be concerned with political matters, but at the same time there may well be a poor personal relationship between the MP and the local party, perhaps stretching back to the time of selection. In addition, as we have seen, local voters and local party supporters may not see the same issues as important, or may hold conflicting attitudes on matters of party policy.

Recent discussion of the position of MPs, especially in cases where disputes have arisen has concentrated on two separate but related questions. First, how effective is the selection process in choosing candidates? Secondly, is it democratic? Both Taverne and Nicolson, in dispute with their local parties on political issues, defended their independence but at the same time acknowledged, with Burke, the ultimate right of their supporters to dismiss them. But before they would accept such dismissal, they demanded that the matter should be put to a wider section of the electorate than the local party committee which had selected them in the first place. The basis of this demand was the belief that the 'party activists' who run the organisation hold more extreme views than the party members as a whole.

Michael Rush's book *The Selection of Parliamentary Candidates* (1969) provides an exhaustive account of the selection procedure in both Labour and Conservative parties. In the Conservative Party, the selection committee consists of a small group of prominent members of the local association. It is the task of this committee to produce a short list from the applications for the candidature received either directly or via Central Office, all of which would usually have been approved by Smith Square in advance. These applications might number as many as 100 in a Conservative-held seat, and would probably average only 50 in a Labour-held seat, with a few hopeless seats attracting no applications at all. After a preliminary list has been drawn up, based on brief biographical details and 'references' from MPs or other prominent Conservatives, some applicants are interviewed. The short list is then produced, with probably three to six names on it. Occasionally, the short list will have only one name.[1] The short list then goes to the Executive Council, which may add to it; if it does so, the addition is usually a local name. The Executive Council holds a selection meeting, at which the possible candidates are required to make a short speech and answer questions. Voting then takes place, the lowest in the ballot being eliminated until someone has an overall majority. A unanimous vote is then usually taken in favour of the successful applicant, and all that remains is for a general meeting of the association to endorse the decision of the Executive Council, though in rare cases it fails to do so.

The corresponding procedure in the Labour Party is both more formal, being laid down in the constitutions of the party and of the CLP, and more complex, reflecting the federated nature of the party. The National Executive Committee also has greater formal powers than Conservative Central Office, though most of these powers are negative in character, and it remains true that local parties of both colours jealously guard their right of candidate selection. Nonetheless, the NEC has power over the initiation of the selection procedure, as well as the power to veto a candidate once selected. As in the Conservative Party, lists of possible candidates are drawn up (one for sponsored and one for unsponsored candidates) but these are in no sense already approved of. The NEC must approve the particular candidate selected, and has sometimes withheld this approval. The number of nominations is more limited than in the Conservative Party, because there is no automatic forwarding of names from party head-quarters. Nominations may come from organisations affiliated to the constituency party, or from party branches who are allowed one each. Information available on the possible candidates is very brief, indeed it is 'often felt to be totally inadequate' (Rush, 1969, p. 155). When all the nominations, rarely more than twenty, have been received, the Executive Committee draws up a short list, sometimes after preliminary inter-viewing. This list usually has five or six names on it. A special General Management Committee meeting is held to approve this list, and then, on a separate occasion, the GMC, sitting as a selection conference, hears the nominees make speeches and answer questions in a way very similar to the Conservative procedure.

Each delegate to the meeting is provided in advance with short bio-graphical details of the nominees, but the selection theoretically depends on the performance of the possible candidates and no discussion is

[1]Sir Gerald Nabarro was selected at Kidderminster in 1964; his was the only name on the list. Another example is Teddy Taylor, selected at Glasgow Cathcart in 1964, following a dispute between the local association and the previous MP, Henderson.

allowed. Voting takes place in the same way as in the Conservative party and when a majority is gained by one nominee, it is usual to pass unanimously a resolution assuring him of the support of the CLP.

Superficially, therefore, the procedures in the two major parties are fairly similar; but selection in the Labour Party is far more complex, because of the role of the trade unions, both nationally sponsoring candidates, and locally, affiliating to CLPs and nominating candidates.

Two general comments may be made. First, selection committees in safe seats – those who are in effect choosing the MP – are those most inexperienced in selecting candidates. When an MP dies or retires, the selection may be the first new one which has been made for many years. Secondly, and this sums up most of the criticism that has been made of the process:

> It would be difficult to devise a method by which fewer people are involved or less knowledge of aspirants is assured than the present system (Richard Rose, 1976, p. 259).

Not surprisingly, unsuitable choices are sometimes made. Peter Paterson recounts how in one constituency, Rochester and Chatham, in the 1950s, both parties picked candidates who seemed quite unsuitable. The Labour candidate, Anne Kerr, was a fervent opponent of nuclear weapons – hardly the most obvious choice for a constituency heavily dependent on defence spending. The local Conservative association, whose Executive consisted mainly of small businessmen, chose Julian Critchley, who favoured abolition of Resale Price Maintenance (1967, pp. 85–6).

Choices can at times be almost random. Paterson mentions the case of a stranger visiting a town on business, who was approached by two local Labour Party members as a possible candidate; the aim was to prevent the selection of the mayor. The newcomer was indeed selected, and later became a 'most capable and energetic Member' (Paterson, 1967, p. 9). The Conservative Party finds the selection procedure satisfactory in most cases. Nigel Nicolson described the reasons for his selection as superficial, and it may be the case that had the committee that selected him known more about his political views, they might have chosen someone else. But lack of information is not necessarily a cause for concern to Conservative selectors. As one party worker put it,

> Most selection committees prefer evils they do not know to evils they know only too well. And if you have two or more local contenders you can create a good deal of ill-will locally by choosing one over the others. In a situation like that it is much better to pass over *all* local contenders and adopt an outsider. (Quoted in Ranney, 1965, p. 110.)

The Conservatives thus place greater emphasis on choosing the 'right sort of person'; specific political views are less important than in the Labour Party. The choice is generally made on strength as a public speaker, and personality, and the system of application rather than nomination gives the local association a fairly wide range of people to choose from. They are more concerned with the circumstances of each particular selection, and with a satisfactory result, and less concerned about the *method* of selection.

The same is not true of the Labour Party. And the rash of disputes between MPs and their local parties in the early 1970s, which preceded the start of the reselection campaign, and indeed gave it much of its ammunition, may well have reflected not only the changes taking place within the party, which will be examined in Chapter 5, but also the faults of the selection process itself. First, information is often totally inadequate. Potential candidates, as in the Conservative Party, may be virtually unknown to the selectors; in some cases all nominees may be complete strangers to the selection conference.

The selection process may not reveal much about them either. No discussion of the merits of the nominees is allowed during the meeting. One former Labour MP described his selection as 'a hit-and-miss affair', and attributed his success to 'speaking ability on the night', the fact that he lived on the edge of the constituency, and a couple of votes from Co-operative delegates (Paul Rose, 1981, p. 25). The procedure has been described as 'in some ways designed to conceal rather than reveal the basic political attitudes of the nominee' (Janosik, 1968, p. 154). More information, more time and a wider choice would all help to improve the process.

One difference between the Labour and Conservative parties is of course the sponsorship of Labour candidates by trade unions. This not only complicates the procedures, but also may lead to the choice of someone who has never visited the district before. A study of Sheffield politics found that in 1966, of six MPs, three were strangers to the city when nominated, and the unions that sponsored them had little connection with the city either (Hampton, 1970, Chapter 4). A local man on the short list may be turned down, not only for reasons similar to those in the Conservative Party quoted above, but also because of the offer of sponsorship for a man no one knows, and few CLPs can afford to disregard the financial benefits of this.

Sponsorship, though primarily a financial arrangement, can be seen as raising a problem of sectionalism. Younger, abler men may be prevented from getting into Parliament because the selectors are likely to choose a sponsored candidate who is more like themselves, but of lesser ability than other contenders. Certainly in the past, trade union MPs were 'awarded' their seats after long careers in their unions. This particular effect of the selection process results from the federated nature of the party and 'many of the cross pressures which affect the selectors are the direct result' of this (Rush, 1969, p. 277).

As an *effective* method of choosing parliamentary candidates and MPs the system is therefore open to more than a few criticisms. But it has also been criticised for its undemocratic nature. First, the selectors are a tiny proportion of the paid-up membership of the party and an even smaller proportion of those who vote for it at elections. Secondly, the selectors, being by definition 'activists', are likely to hold views which are unrepresentative of the rest of the voters. These criticisms are not especially new ones. Ostrogorski discerned that those most active in the caucus were likely to hold more extreme views, and in more recent times Nicolson made the same accusation against his opponents in Bournemouth. Recently, the same charge has been made about Labour Party activists, especially since the success of the reselection campaign.

The first of these criticisms, that very few members of a CLP or local Conservative association take part in the selection of parliamentary candidates, seems to be undeniably true. Although Conservative associations tend to have a higher membership than local Labour parties, in a non-Conservative held seat, membership may be as low as 1000. Even where the membership is larger, those who take part in the selection will be a tiny proportion of the total membership, perhaps as low as 1 per cent. In the Labour Party, ordinary members do not even have the opportunity – which is on occasion in the Conservative Party rather more than a formality – of endorsing the candidate at a General Meeting.[1] In the Labour Party, similarly, selection is the prerogative of a relatively small group of the membership. This is in spite of the fact that, far more than the Conservatives, the Labour Party subscribes to the ideal of democratic methods. After the nomination stage, practically all the membership is excluded. The mandating of delegates is frowned upon, if not a direct contravention of the rules. As a result,

'Most MPs today are thus effectively selected by fewer voters than in the days before the 1832 Reform Act.' (Richard Rose, 1976, p. 252.)

This in itself might be sufficient reason for opening up the 'secret garden' of British politics; but if activists, who run the party and select the candidate, are extremists in their political views then there is all the more reason for changing the procedure so as to reflect the opinions of a wider section of the party.

In fact survey evidence does not entirely bear this out. Activists in both

---

[1]Rush (1969, p. 53) mentions eight cases between 1952 and 1963 when the General Meeting refused endorsement. In all of these, local men were involved, but in only two was the move successful.

parties share a strong attachment to their own party and an equally strong dislike for the other side, and Labour Party activists, unlike the deferential Conservatives, also have a deep suspicion of their own party leadership at all levels, 'from the leader and the NEC down to the local executive' (Ranney, 1965, p. 177). In spite of this, several studies have found that activists are 'not homogeneously extremist and some are not even strongly partisan' (Richard Rose, 1976, pp. 207–8). Activists often disagree amongst themselves, and many of their values and their motives for becoming involved in politics are not partisan. Thus, if not passive followers of the leadership, they are not necessarily forces for extremism.

On the other hand, there are two important factors that have affected the Labour Party in recent years. One is the development of a gap – a yawning gulf – between the ideas of activists and those of ordinary Labour voters on party policy. The latter often disagree with most of the contents of a Labour manifesto, preferring in fact the policies put forward by Conservative MPs (Rose, 1976). Secondly, Labour Party membership is exceedingly low. A study of the Labour left, published in 1966, included the following remark:

> For every keen and eloquent activist there are a dozen or more citizens who appear to be virtually apolitical apart from a basic loyalty to the Labour movement in general. (Ian Aitken 'The Structure of the Labour Party' in Kaufman (ed.), 1966.)

Since that time the number of individual members of the party has fallen significantly. The dozen solid citizens may now be reduced to a mere half-dozen. And it is this lack of members rather than any small group of extremists, which have always been present in most local Labour parties, which is at the heart of the problem. By 1971, the average official membership of a CLP had fallen to five or six hundred, but many were much smaller, and were beginning to have the character of closed groups. Ron Hayward said in 1972, when he took over as secretary of the party:

> Some parties don't want new members. They have got a nice comfortable little clique and don't want new faces to upset them. (Quoted in R. Rose, p. 153.)

It is this exclusiveness which threatens the representative nature of the local party and its selection process. Parties that have tiny memberships are vulnerable to 'infiltration'; if all the activists hold 'extreme' views, then the CLPs will become small sects which have no real roots in the community of which they are supposed to form part. Reform of the selection procedures might serve to revitalise the party; one proposal is to introduce some form of primary election so as to include all the members. This is a subject which will be dealt with in Chapter 10.

4 The Labour Party and representation – background

The dilemmas which face all MPs in defining their relationships with the party nationally, with the constituency party, its members and activists, and with the electorate at large, are especially acute for those in the Labour Party. Uncertainty about how much freedom of action they retain, and how far they are controlled by the party, is much greater for Labour MPs than for those who represent other parties. The reasons for this can be found in the history of the party – in its origins in the working-class movement outside Parliament, in the persistent ambiguities which go back to the very foundation of the party, and in its ideology. All have contributed to the perennial conflicts which the party has experienced, and all have affected MPs and their relations with the rest of the party.

The origins of the Labour Party are very different from those of the Conservative and Liberal parties. The enlargement of the electorate at the end of the nineteenth century meant that the House of Commons was no longer a closed society and that contemporary politicians had to seek the support of the new voters. Both the Conservatives and the Liberals formed extra-parliamentary organisations for this purpose, but attempts by Randolph Churchill and Joseph Chamberlain to democratise their respective parties and make the parliamentary leadership accountable to the rank and file in the country proved ultimately unsuccessful, and the organisations remained merely vote-getting agencies. By contrast, the Labour Party started outside Parliament. When the first Labour MPs took their seats, they were extending into Parliament a working-class movement which was already successful in the country. From the beginning, therefore, Labour MPs were seen as the 'servants of the movement' and in consequence subject to extra-parliamentary control. As well as this, Labour was founded as a class party; its expressed purpose was to represent the working class in Parliament. The working class was assumed to be a homogeneous group with common interests, which the MPs were delegated to represent. The concept of the representative as a delegate was already familiar to both the trade unionists and the socialists in the infant party.

The new party's constitution endowed its conference with supreme authority as a policy-making body. The formal constitutional arrangements thus enshrined the principle of   extra-parliamentary control. Labour MPs then and now have not only the dilemma of reconciling the still-powerful notion of an independent representative with the discipline of a modern party, but have the added difficulty of being subjected to policy making by an external body. These problems are theoretically resolved by the doctrine of the mandate. In practice the position of a Labour MP remains confused, as it has been through the party's history. To whom are Labour MPs responsible? To the Conference? To the NEC? To the local party? To the electorate as a whole? The constitution of the party has provided an opportunity for the perpetuation of its disputes; because of the different power centres within the party, it has always been possible to re-open any conflict, and issues have never been clearly settled.

The adoption in 1918 of a socialist ideology provided even greater opportunities for disagreement. The very existence of such articles of faith presupposed a common view of the party's aims and objects. It demanded that all members of the party should share 'an identity of views and unanimity of purpose' (Beer, 1965, p. 239). But disagreement on the exact meaning and content of the ideology has been rife. And since the party is also committed to democratic methods, the result has been continuous controversy.

The party in the country, in particular the constituency party activists, whose importance was discussed in Chapter 3, has often during the party's history been in dispute with the leadership on all of these four points: the seat of power, the meaning of socialism, and the importance of class as well as the extent to which MPs should take instructions.

The party leadership, usually identified with the right and often supported by the big trade unions, has generally been successful in escaping from the tight control by Conference implied by the party constitution. From time to time the left has gained greater influence, most notably since 1970. But none of the issues raised by the left since that time are new ones; on the contrary, they have bedevilled the party since its inception. The campaign for reselection must be seen as part of a desire to return to fundamentals. The determination to exert greater control over the elected representatives of the party goes together with the reassertion of the authority of conference, and the insistence on socialist policies and the importance of class. An understanding of the historical points of conflict is necessary as a background to considering the campaign for reselection, which will be dealt with in succeeding chapters.

The Labour Representation Committee founded in 1900, was a coalition of trade unions and the much weaker socialist societies, the ILP,

Fabians and SDF.[1] Although the LRC was a step forward for the trade unionists (see Miliband, 1961, p. 17) it was, in a sense, a step back for the ILP, which was joining a group which had no commitment to socialism at all; though it was a short-cut it gave the party a built-in weakness, a division between 'reformers' and 'revolutionaries' which persists to the present day. The socialists were already in a minority: the rest of the LRC were 'enmeshed in the intellectual and ideological universe of Liberal–Radicalism' (D. Coates, 1975, p. 9). Most members of the new party were trade unionists, and as a result the practices and procedures which it adopted were derived from trade unionism. Most significantly for this analysis, these included the mandating of delegates and the idea of conference supremacy; other historical legacies from trade unionism included egalitarianism and a distrust of the leadership.

If the trade union element in the LRC was likely to hold a delegate view of representation, this was also true of the socialists, even in the very earliest days. Even before 1918 the extra-parliamentary party was frequently dissatisfied with its parliamentary representatives and for reasons which are strikingly similar to those heard again in the 1970s and early 1980s. As early as 1902,

> The socialist activists in the party could not reconcile themselves to the notion that their parliamentarians should enjoy a Burkean kind of independence. The parliamentarians, on the other hand, wanted the greatest possible degree of freedom in their political activities.

Miliband sees this as the expression of a purely ideological difference of view. He goes on:

> These divergent attitudes had very little to do with abstract principles concerning the proper working of parliamentary government or the rights and duties of Members of Parliament. Underlying the tension between activists and parliamentarians was the former's fear that the Labour group in Parliament would, if it were not strictly controlled, backslide into opportunism, manoeuvre and compromise, and the latter's easy assumption that manoeuvre and compromise were inherent in their situation and essential to the furtherance of Labour's immediate aims (1961, p. 26).

Thus, in many ways, little has changed in eighty years.

The claim of Labour members for independence derived from several sources; they wanted to be re-elected, to have greater flexibility in parliamentary tactics and more strength as a group in the House. This desire was reinforced by the pattern set by the older parties, as well as by the rules

---

[1]The SDF had left the LRC by 1906, when the organisation, now supported by many more unions, changed its name to the Labour Party.

of parliamentary privilege and the influence of the Whig theory of the constitution.

After the 1906 election when for the first time a sizeable number of Labour MPs entered the House and were conceded autonomy in the management of their own affairs, a clarification of the relationship with the extra-parliamentary party became more urgent. Hence the passing of a resolution on the matter at the 1907 Annual Conference, which read:

> That resolutions instructing the parliamentary party as to their action in the House of Commons be taken as the opinion of the Conference on the understanding that the time and method of giving effect to these instructions be left to the party in the House, in conjunction with the National Executive Committee.

This resolution confirmed the conference as having the right to instruct the parliamentary party, though leaving the right to decide priorities to the leadership. The latter was thus in effect more or less independent. It also:

> greatly enhanced the activists' faith in the efficacy of conference resolutions and their ineradicable conviction that the passage of resolutions at annual conferences must automatically entail important consequences in regard to Party policy (Miliband, 1961, p. 277).

The 1907 resolution was clearly open to different interpretations: that most revered of Labour leaders, Keir Hardie, refused to accept instructions from anyone as to his conduct in the House, a stand often mentioned later by embattled parliamentarians. It was the failure of the parliamentary leadership under Wilson to take account of Conference which amongst other causes led to the CLPD campaign for reselection in the 1970s.

Before 1918, the Labour party could have been described as 'a Parliamentary expression of trade union aspirations which involved no coherent programme and no officially accepted socialist commitment' (D. Coates, 1975, p. 14). From that year the party committed itself to a socialist ideology. With an enormous growth in trade union membership, the time had come to split away from a close alliance with the Liberals, who were reluctant to share their power. The new ideology served to distinguish Labour as an independent political party, aiming to establish itself as a separate power in the nation. Class was a very important element in this: 'A class – or more precisely the organised section of a class – was asserting its claim to power.' (Beer, 1965, p. 152.) Once Labour aimed to be a party of government, as it did after 1918, problems were bound to arise with the delegate concept of representation.

The party was also reorganised: the conference remained the sovereign body of the party with the trade unions becoming the main power centre of the party, both at the conference and on the NEC. The socialist societies lost their special allocation of NEC seats and the whole conference was to elect each NEC member. Constituency Labour parties were set up, transforming what had been a loose federation into a nationally cohesive party with individual membership. But as far as party structure and authority were concerned, the ambiguities of the 1907 resolution were enshrined in the 1918 Constitution.

While the new Constitution stated that it was 'the duty of every parliamentary representative of the party to be guided by the decision of the meetings of such parliamentary representatives, with a view to giving effect to the decisions of the Party Conference', there was flexibility in this and the PLP was accorded a joint role in the preparation of the manifesto. Nor were the boundaries of authority between the PLP, the NEC and the conference at all clearly defined.

If the minority Socialist group had less prominence under the new scheme of things, its needs were met by Clause IV of the new Constitution, the declaration that Labour was a socialist party, and by the 1918 programme 'Labour and the New Social Order'. The tensions that already existed in the party, strengthened by the lack of clear authority resulting from the party's structure, were exacerbated by the adoption of the new programme and the commitment to socialism, even though many of the items in the document had previously been accepted as resolutions by conference.

> The establishment of a programme and goal gradually widened the scope of intra-party conflict and raised, in more acute form, questions of electoral, parliamentary and governmental tactics, and thus increased the likehood of disagreement over authority in the Party. (Minkin, 1978, p. 9.)

This conflict followed factional lines: put very simply it was between those who held a 'militant–visionary' view and those who held a pragmatic short-term one, between those who felt specifically socialist policies were essential and those who did not. The Left–Right ideological split has since dominated all other conflicts, and though the right-wing MPs and left-wing activists represented the extremes, this was not merely a conflict between the leadership and the rank and file, but spread vertically through all levels of the party (see Beer, 1965, p. 231). The ideological divisions within the party reinforced those on conference authority, and the extent of power to be accorded to the parliamentary party.

> For both instrumental and ideological reasons the Right was generally in favour of more independence for the PLP, the Left in favour of less. (Minkin, 1978, p. 11.)

There was always, however, a substantial 'centrist' section, both in the PLP and in the trade unions, so that outright confrontation and clarification of the issue of authority were usually avoided.

In general, the parliamentary leadership retained the ascendancy and escaped from rigorous control by the Conference; an important factor in this was the growing personal authority of the leader of the party throughout the mass organisation. Most notably in the MacDonald years, power shifted to the leadership. The first Labour government in 1924 worked hard to educate the Labour movement 'into the meaning of political orthodoxy and into a keener sense of the national interest' (Miliband, 1961, p. 105). But the left, sometimes as deferentially loyal as the right, continued for a long time to feel that MacDonald was one of themselves, an experience repeated thirty years later when Harold Wilson assumed the leadership. A 1929 amendment to the Constitution reflected the greater independence of the PLP, in that MP's duties were no longer specified.

The debacle of 1931 resulted in great hostility in the party in the country to the parliamentary leadership and a reassertion of party control over MPs; or at least 'a reaffirmation of the basic formula of 1907' (Minkin, 1978b, p. 19). The Attlee years saw a greater effort by the leadership to adjust to extra-parliamentary opinion. The left remained weak; one major reason for this was that they were so vulnerable to the criticism of 'rocking the boat' (Miliband, 1961, p. 32). The early Labour governments, under MacDonald particularly but also later under Harold Wilson, went out of their way to prove themselves a 'national' party, to demonstrate their moderation, reponsibility and fitness to rule. The dilemma of the left is well summed up by David Coates, 1975 (pp. 200–201).

> The very organisation of a left-wing faction within the Labour Party threatened the unity, and through that, the electoral viability of the Party to whose electoral success the left was itself committed . . . too explicit an organisation for left-wing causes invariably alienated the very party leadership that the left-wing sought to influence. For left-wing activism could be – and invariably was – seen by the leadership of the party as a challenge to its authority. (Coates, 1975, pp. 200–201.)

Weak not only in Parliament, but also in Conference, where union block votes generally supported the leadership, a second dilemma presented itself for those who felt that MPs should be delegates of the Conference, but at the same time did not agree with many Conference decisions.

Even in 1945, before the famous victory which the party was to win in the first general election for ten years, when the left was more powerful than it had been for a long time, it failed to achieve a great deal in its own terms. The nationalisation proposals in *Let us Face the Future*, the campaign document, represented 'the least the Executive could present to the Conference without causing acute dissension in the party' and indeed less than had been agreed a year before. The left, lacking coherence and organisation, as always, was not prepared 'on the eve of an election to challenge the leadership' (Miliband, 1961, p. 280). Beneath the pre-election unanimity, however, the party was as deeply divided as ever. According to the Nuffield election study for 1945:

> There was a striking difference of tone between the speeches of the leaders and the rank and file of the party. The leaders tended to restrain, while their followers urged them to go further in their policy of socialism. (McCallum and Redman, 1947, p. 129.)

The very success of the Attlee government of 1945–51, with its large nationalisation programme and the introduction of the NHS revealed the inadequacies of 'Labourism' for the left of the party, which was faced again with the basic question of reform or revolution:

> Whether the Labour Party is to be concerned with attempts at a more efficient and humane administration of a capitalist society; or whether it is to adapt itself to the task of creating a socialist one. (Miliband, 1961, p. 344.)

The thirteen years in opposition which followed Labour's 1951 election defeat were marked, especially after their second defeat in 1955, and Gaitskell's assumption of the leadership, by a shift to the right. The Conservatives did not dismantle the welfare state or de-nationalise most of the industries taken into public ownership between 1945 and 1951. These were the 'You've never had it so good' years of Harold Macmillan, and as R. H. S. Crossman saw, the party was 'being ideologically disintegrated by the fact that Keynesian welfare capitalism was proving for the time being, quite an adequate substitute for socialism'. Another view, that of a left-winger untempered by office, was that the party had:

> moved away from the class perspectives and the socialist rhetoric which had buttressed the aspirations of the inter-war generation and downgraded in importance the policy initiatives through which in 1945 the Labour Party had attempted to realise its inter-war potential and promise (D. Coates, 1975, p. 76).

Gaitskell was committed to what became known as the new revisionism. His election accentuated the rightward shift and gave it a 'much sharper ideological and political articulation' (Miliband, 1961, p. 332). The Bevanite struggles of the early 1950s were for the moment hidden rather than revealed. There was no strong or specific commitment to further large scale nationalisation; it now seemed to be an electoral liability and irrelevant; socialism was now more about equality, and a classless society. A third defeat in the 1959 election resulted in the revisionist line being further developed; Gaitskell went so far as to attack the sacred Clause IV. 'Revisionism', as many commentators have described, included several elements and leaned heavily on academic findings.

The decline of the manual working class and the theory of *embourgeoisement* were two important arguments; more relevant for our purposes is the discovery (Minkin, 1978b, p. 276) that 'the activist appeared to be on the point of organisational redundancy'. The Nuffield election study of 1959 indicated that local organisation had little impact on election results and that any impression on the voter was more likely to be made by the mass media, especially television. Politicians now appealed directly to the voters and the party worker's role as an intermediary seemed to be less important. On this analysis, the activists were less necessary for the politicians' purposes than they had been in the past; these activists were thought to be keen to take part in policy making, in a sense a reward for their hard work on the doorsteps. If the latter was no longer required, perhaps the former could also be dispensed with.

How far these considerations were voiced remains a matter of debate, but it seems fairly clear that the proponents of revisionism disliked the traditional procedures of the Labour Party – the mandating of delegates etc. – which they saw as anachronistic. Participatory democracy was not highly valued; indeed, a fear of mass activism was common. The leading revisionist theoretician, Anthony Crosland, showed a strong distaste for activism, and saw in it a 'real threat to the stability of our democracy' (quoted in Minkin, 1978b, p. 277).

Years later, in spite of a widespread feeling in favour of participation by ordinary people in the decisions which affect their lives, these feelings still remained, though they were less forcefully expressed; for instance an editorial in *Socialist Commentary* (October 1975) stressed that it is what is done at national level which really matters, and deprecated too much stress on the importance of activists in the constituencies.

These views naturally complemented the long-standing desire of the majority of the PLP for independence; electoral failure and the consequent attempt to appeal to the widest possible section of the electorate by moderating traditional Labour policies led to major clashes with conference and a re-opening of the old debate. Gaitskell's attack on Clause IV in 1959 and his defeat the following year on unilateral nuclear disarmament revealed the divisions in the party once more.

At the 1960 Scarborough conference, the day before Gaitskell's impassioned 'fight, fight and fight again' speech, a debate took place which was perhaps as important in the long term as the Clause 4 debate on the right of conference to determine policy and issue instructions to the PLP. The resolutions debated had been put down in anticipation of Gaitskell's defiance of the conference on the unilateralist issue.[1] A strongly worded resolution, the mover of which admitted that he wanted to 'bind our Parliamentary Party hand and foot', was defeated; a second resolution, moved by John Stonehouse MP, was accepted with reservations by the NEC and passed by conference. The resolution acknowledged that 'the day-to-day tactics in Parliament must be the job of the Parliamentary Labour Party', but declared 'that Labour policy is decided by the Party Conference which is the final authority'. In moving the resolution, Stonehouse said that it was not the wish of its promoters to subject MPs to detailed instructions, 'for that would be unconstitutional', but at the same time they must not defy Conference.

The reply on behalf of the NEC was given by A.L. Williams, Deputy General Secretary of the Party; he insisted that the PLP could not act on instructions from any body, but that 'the PLP could not for long remain at loggerheads with annual Conference without disrupting the party', and added '... in a democratic movement we do not even talk about instructions; we meet new situations by consultation, by an attempt to get the greatest measure of agreement'. Not surprisingly, 'the debate ended in absolute confusion' (Minkin, 1978b, p. 280), but the scene had been set for Gaitskell's defiance of conference the following day.

The question of authority within the party, as well as the issue of unilateralism, was fiercely debated over the succeeding months. The debate over party authority could be seen as being on two levels:

> On one level it was about the rights of Conference and the rights of Members of Parliament; it was about the proper relationship between a representative, his party and his constituency; it was about the Party's constitution and the British constitution; and it was about individual representation and class representation. For the more radical on the Right of the Party, however, it was about something more fundamental – the modernisation of the Party, its organisation, purpose and strategy... a rejection of the kind of politics involved in mass party activism and intra-party democracy. (Minkin, 1978b, p. 281.)

Both levels of the argument are relevant to the issues raised by mandatory reselection.

There were inconsistencies on both sides. The left, which had claimed the right to dissent, now appeared to be denying that right to the Gaitskellites. It was now a majority of the PLP which did not agree with the Conference decision, and Gaitskell argued that they should be allowed to disagree and campaign for the reversal of the decision: 'The right to dissent is not something that can be made to depend on the fewness of

[1]See McKenzie, 1963, p. 617 ff, for a very full account.

those who dissent. It must be allowed to the majority.'

Some Bevanites in the PLP attempted to draw a distinction between the authority of conference when Labour was in opposition and when it was in government. But Gaitskell secured his position well before the 1961 Conference. He soon mobilised a majority on the NEC as well as in the PLP and was also supported by the General Council of the TUC; he also defeated Harold Wilson who stood against him in the leadership election. Gaitskell's defiance had only enhanced his power and prestige in the party: a clear lesson to future party leaders. The clashes of 1959 and 1960 paved the way for the breakdown of conference authority when Labour was in government from 1964 to 1970 and for the demands of party activists to control their parliamentary representatives which was to follow. The election of Harold Wilson as Labour's leader in 1963 after Gaitskell's sudden death provided a healing touch. He received the support of all left-wing Labour MPs and of *Tribune*; one MP said, 'In Harold Wilson we have a leader fully worthy of the tradition of Clem Attlee and Keir Hardie'. (Walter Padley, quoted in Foot, 1968, p. 302.) By the time he became Prime Minister in 1964, Wilson had succeeded in uniting the party and its affiliates as it had not been united since 1945; there was even enthusiasm from the *New Left Review*. It may be that the adulation Wilson received from the entire party contributed to the extent of the disillusion which was to follow. The government's first few months were taken up with constant sterling crises. In spite of the financial situation, one of its first actions was to abolish prescription charges in fulfilment of a manifesto commitment. The Commons majority of only three made tight parliamentary discipline imperative. Government support for American bombing in Vietnam and the 1965 Immigration White Paper, as well as the necessity to shelve the proposed steel nationalisation after the revolt by two Labour back-benchers, Donnelly and Wyatt, may have given Wilson's left-wing supporters cause for concern, but the overwhelming victory at the general election in March 1966 gave rise to renewed hope that the party might introduce more socialist policies.

The euphoria of victory was to evaporate after only a few months. Faced with heavy pressure on the pound and a seamen's strike, a severe deflationary package was introduced in July 1966 which included a six-month statutory wage freeze. This was followed by a period of 'severe restraint', ending in July 1967, but the balance of payments continued to worsen and finally the government was forced to devalue the pound. Further cuts in public expenditure followed, including the reimposition of prescription charges. Wilson's ill-fated attempt to take Britain into the Common Market was a further failure. The goverment's standing in the country, reflected in unprecedented by-election losses, could hardly have been worse, and the Prime Minister's relations with the party, in and out of Parliament, deteriorated sharply. They were exacerbated by such incidents as the efforts by some in the Cabinet to lift the ban on sales of arms to South Africa, as well as the failure to repudiate US policy in Vietnam, the government's policy of allowing sales to the federal side in the Nigeria/Biafra war, and the slowness of the withdrawal of forces from East of Suez. Rising unemployment during 1968 did not improve matters.

All of these developments resulted in the alienation not only of many in the CLPs and the unions, but also of a large section on the left of the PLP. Defeats in conference increased, reaching a peak in 1968; opposition to the government was deepest on prescription charges and incomes policy. Also, for the first time in the party's history, relations between the NEC and the government became problematic. Wilson's firm insistence that 'the government must govern', with none of the face-saving forms of words used to mask disagreement in the Attlee years, angered and disillusioned the mass of the party in the country.

Finally, early in 1969, the White Paper *In Place of Strife* was published. These proposals for trade union reform were seen by many Labour party supporters as 'the last straw' (Taverne, 1974, p. 43). The opposition to them of a large number of the parliamentary party, on the right as well as on the left, played an important part, perhaps even a crucial one, in the decision to abandon the proposals. But the hostility of the NEC and the General Council of the TUC were a vital part of the background to the position of many MPs on the issue; 'Protecting "the Movement" became a major consideration for many MPs who would normally have given the Government loyal support' (Minkin, 1978b, p. 307).

Although *In Place of Strife* was a high watermark of resistance by the Labour Party as a whole to the government, in which the parliamentary party played its part, from the time of the July measures of 1966 the Labour left in Parliament had been in almost permanent opposition. The large majority – ninety-seven – with which Labour had been returned to power meant that discipline was likely to be a problem; from 1964 to 1966, with a tiny majority it had been possible to keep all the back-benchers firmly to the leadership's line, except on steel nationalisation. Now the protestors could not be whipped so easily into the government lobby, and the many large backbench rebellions with which the government had to deal over the next three years underlined clearly the divisions within the party and demonstrated vividly the dilemmas that face Labour MPs.

Parliamentary dissent, however, had been a feature of the party since its earliest days, in spite or because of the commitment to strong discipline. The LRC had from the very beginning seen firm discipline as essential: even before the first sizeable group of Labour members arrived after the General Election of 1906, it had declared (at the 1902 Conference – see McKenzie, 1963, p. 388) that all candidates must pledge themselves to accept the party constitution and 'to abide by the decisions of the group in carrying out the aims of the constitution or resign'. At this stage there were only three members in the House, all dependent on the LRC financially, for in those days MPs were still unpaid. After 1906, however, with twenty-nine Labour members in the House, the question of discipline became more important and the very strict line taken four years earlier was already modified; it was no longer necessary to resign when not in agreement with the majority of the PLP. A conscience clause was introduced in 1906 when one MP was reluctant, for religious reasons, to vote with the rest of the group on the Education Bill. Ever since, the extent of freedom granted by such clauses has been a matter of dispute within the party. The left have often found themselves in the difficult position of favouring firm discipline in theory but in practice disagreeing with the majority of the parliamentary party, and therefore demanding the right to dissent. The right, conversely, favouring greater independence for MPs, have sometimes found themselves in the awkward situation of demanding firmer discipline.

The first two Labour governments, under Ramsay MacDonald, were in constant difficulty with the left-wingers in the party. The first, in 1924, was dependent on Liberal votes and thus forced 'to compromise its socialist principles' (Butt, 1967, p. 116), and as a result was under constant attack from the back-benches. By the time of the second MacDonald government in 1929, the conscience clause was interpreted more narrowly, and did not permit voting against a party decision. But with the ILP truly 'a party within a party' the PLP was in complete disarray in any case. The Attlee government of 1945–51 did not have serious problems of discipline; those that arose were principally concerned with defence and foreign affairs. But there was a marked difference between this and the situation under MacDonald. He had seen criticism as treachery, while Attlee's premiership was characterised by the view that criticism should be dealt with rather than suppressed; the same attitude informed the government's dealings with conference. Once out of office, however, after 1951, discipline was more firmly administered as the Bevanite rebellions threatened party unity. These were usually on defence matters. One revolt in 1955 involved sixty-two MPs and was 'too large to be disciplined' (Miliband, 1961, p. 239), but as a result the standing orders of the PLP were redrafted in sterner form. The conscience clause was tightened up; it no longer permitted members to vote against the decision of a party meeting. 'Conscience,' Attlee said 'should be a still, small voice and not a loudspeaker.'

Problems of parliamentary discipline then were perennial, in spite of the traditional commitment to being a far more regulated party than the Conservatives. One can discern a pattern of swings from more liberal to tougher regimes, then a clamp-down when revolts became too common, or too threatening to the leadership. The situation in 1966–70 was different, however, in several ways from what had been experienced in the past. First, the size of the rebellions: very large numbers of abstentions were commonplace, not just isolated incidents as before. The hard-core of rebels in 1951–5 was only eight in number; during the 1966–70 government, the Whips became accustomed to far larger numbers than that defying them. Secondly, previously the few large-scale abstentions – apart from a rebellion on conscription in 1947 – had taken place when Labour was in opposition, not in government.

The third difference in 1966–70 was that the new intake of Labour MPs after the election, more than seventy in number, was not like its predecessors. More of them came from university and professional backgrounds – 'too many mortar-boards and not enough cloth caps' said one critic – and their political attitudes were more questioning and intransigent; they had high expectations of Parliament's duties and rewards. They also included more younger, better educated working-class members. Wilson himself wrote, in his memoirs of the period that 'there had never up to that time been an intake which looked less like lobby fodder'. During 1966, as the government took ever more unpopular decisions – notably the wage freeze – back-benchers became increasingly disillusioned and rebellious. Richard Crossman and John Silkin were appointed Leader of the House and Chief Whip respectively and decided to 'run the parliamentary party on a light rein' (Foot, 1968, p. 312), recalling perhaps Bevan's dictum that 'a firmer lid is hardly the recipe for a boiling pot'. The conscience clause, it was decided, would be interpreted in a relaxed way. Crossman wrote later:

> We would have to realise that when a government suddenly does things which are not in the party manifesto and which are profoundly controversial, then Members have the right to challenge that government and in the last resort to abstain conscientiously. (Crossman, 1976, Vol. II, p. 95.)

The corollary of this was that no 'party within a party' would be tolerated; 'conscience must be individual, not collective, not organised' (Crossman, 1976, Vol. II, p. 96). But a fresh revolt on the Prices and Incomes Bill angered the loyalists in the PLP, who wanted the Whip withdrawn from the rebels. This Silkin refused to initiate; it would play into the hands of the Conservative opposition and might even result in a party split. This remained the abiding fear; the size of the opposition on the backbenches to so many aspects of the government's policy meant that no real discipline could be exerted. Steps were taken, however, to placate the right wing of the party. A ban on organised groups within the party, first brought in under Attlee in the days of the Bevanite revolts, was reintroduced. This had little impact, and on several occasions the right wing of the PLP protested against the lenient treatment of the left, by themselves abstaining instead of going into the government lobby. In March 1967, Wilson, who soon wanted a favourable vote on the EEC, made his famous dog licence speech to the PLP:

> All I say is, 'watch it'! Every dog is allowed one bite, but a different view is taken of a dog that goes on biting all the time – things happen to that dog – he may not get his licence renewed when it falls due.

Wilson's contempt only hardened the resolve of the rebels; in the Common Market vote, thirty-six voted against the government and about fifty abstained. The reprimands of the Whips stressed the distinction between an act of conscience and one of hostility; and a new code of conduct was produced which included a rewritten conscience clause which gave MPs no right to vote against the decision of a party meeting. There was an unsuccessful attempt to include a provision which would have absolved MPs from obeying the Whips if they were following conference decisions. Though this came to nothing, the fact that over the next two years there was a series of major rebellions and that the government was forced to abandon its Bill for House of Lords reform as well as the industrial relations proposals indicates that when the government and a large part of the rest of the party, supported by the conference, take such different views on policy, discipline cannot be maintained.

Richard Crossman commented: 'The Labour Party has learnt to tolerate thirty or forty people constantly voting against us whenever they like.' Outside the House, he thought, there had been no ill effects, but 'terrible ill-will' inside it (Crossman, 1977, Vol. III, pp. 414–15). The Whips had for all practical purposes ceased to fulfil their function. A close study of rebels in both parties revealed that:

> Rebels and Whips both think that a private and subtle process of accommodation takes place . . . and that rebellion and discipline are only public symptoms that this process has failed to operate. (Jackson, 1975, p. 200.)

The government's determination to govern in spite of opposition on the back-benches and in the party outside Parliament would have effects in the party as a whole; one of these effects was the rise of the demand for automatic reselection. As Robert McKenzie commented in a more general context, the leadership cannot:

> ignore with impunity the moods and aspirations of their followers; they must carry their followers (and above all their followers in the parliamentary party) with them. And to do so, they have to take into account at every stage the clearly defined currents of opinion within

their party. Blind appeals to loyalty (either to the person of the leader or to the party itself) are frequently resorted to, and often they achieve their purpose. But they are rarely successful in bridging a real gulf when one does develop between the leaders and their followers (1963, p. 644).

The extent of the gulf which existed in the Labour party by 1970, and the consequences which flowed from it are the subject of Chapter 5.

5 Labour and representation: 1970 and after

The party, as well as the country, was disillusioned with the Wilson Government in 1970. For many Labour party members, the government of 1966–70 had been a failure:

> It had revoked its mandate commitments, ignored conference decisions, and carried through policies which ran counter to some of the basic principles of the party. (Minkin, 1978b, p. 330.)

Indeed Wilson's pragmatism and enthusiasm to show that Labour was a party of government had made it difficult for the Conservative opposition to attack him successfully, and the election itself, though it proved to be a close-run thing to the very end of the campaign, indicated little enthusiasm on the part of the electorate for either main party.

Within the Labour movement the loss of enthusiasm had been reflected in a disastrous fall in party membership; the years 1966–70 had been years when the 'grass came away from the roots' in a memorable phrase (Jeger, 1968). Activists were leaving in droves, some to join pressure groups, some to join small left-wing political groups. Individual constituency parties were collapsing; by 1970 the CLP vote at the annual conference was only 11 per cent of the trade union votes. At the same time, however, those activists who had not been driven out by the government's policies voiced their views more loudly and with greater determination than in the past; the grass roots were no longer prepared to accept 'the inferior role assigned to them' (Forester, 1973).

The debates at Labour's annual conference in 1970, following the general election defeat, demonstrated vividly the disillusionment of the rank and file, which had no doubt been exacerbated by the fact that Labour had lost. Also very much in evidence was their determination to be heard. This was reinforced by the vogue for participation which was beginning to make itself felt in many spheres, both local and national. 'Participation' was the subject of a conference debate, which was itself rather bland, but the theme recurred throughout the conference, and particularly in relation to government policies.

The mover of a resolution which called for more nationalisation measures said that the next Labour government must

> avoid the fateful error of ignoring the wishes and voices of the constituencies and affiliated organisations from whom springs the support and strength of the Labour party movement (Labour Party Annual Conference Report 1970, p. 171).

Another speaker called for three basic elements in the party's approach: principle, a programme of radical change, and the return of power to the people. Former ministers, whose policies had been rejected at the recent election, might have been expected to be the targets of criticism, but the rest of the parliamentary party was not spared either. Jack Jones declared, to loud applause:

> For too many MPs, the constituency Labour party is a bit of a nuisance, a device for giving him a free hand as the mood takes him.

He went on,

> For too long the idea has been about that an MP was just a representative and not a delegate . . . in so many cases the MP has not even been a representative (Labour Party Annual Conference Report, 1970, p. 176).

In a debate on conference decisions, delegates discussed the following resolution,

> This conference believes that the Parliamentary Labour Party leaders, whether in government or in opposition, should reflect the views and aspirations of the Labour and trade union movement, by framing their policies on annual conference decisions.
>
> While appreciating that the Parliamentary Labour Party must deal with matters arising in Parliament which have not been the subject of annual conference decision, it deplores the Parliamentary Labour Party's refusal to act on conference decisions. (Labour Party Annual Conference Report 1970, p. 180.)

The proposer of this resolution said that party workers had been 'hurt' by the flouting of conference decisions on five specific issues: prescription charges, Vietnam, unemployment, the wage freeze, and trade union legislation. Pleading for conference decisions to be respected, he begged, 'do not disillusion us'. The seconder of the resolution spoke of the 'increasing apathy and frustration found amongst party workers in the constituencies' caused by the policies of the last government. Another speaker, who described as cynical the way in which the party leadership rejected conference decisions, called MPs elitist and said:

> I do not think we are asking for very much. We are asking that the

broad outlines of party policy should be determined here. I suggest that in addition it is reasonable that we should ask, when it proves impossible, for reasons outside either party or Labour government control, to implement these, that we should be given a reasonable explanation of why it has proved impossible. (Labour Party Annual Conference Report 1970, p. 182.)

Harold Wilson, replying to the debate, asked for the resolution to be remitted. In 1968, on a similar subject, he had said,

Every resolution carried against the platform ... we accept as a warning to the government. A warning, not an instruction. No one has ever seriously claimed that a government which must be responsible to Parliament can be instructed. This was repeatedly said from this platform under the last Labour government (i.e. 1945–51) and never seriously challenged. (Labour Party Annual Conference Report 1968, p. 299.)

Wilson took up the same theme in 1970, claiming that Williams's 1960 Scarborough speech (quoted in Chapter 4 above) had been 'accepted ever since', and he continued:

I cannot imagine any Labour Prime Minister or Labour government, when we have a parliamentary majority, which did not seek to act in accordance with the general policy, and indeed wishes, of this movement. But timing and priorities must be a matter for the government ... (Labour Party Annual Conference Report 1970, p. 184).

Thus restating the terms of the 1907 resolution, Wilson added a gloss which was newer; this was the idea that Labour was now the natural 'party of government', and he rejected the condemnatory tone of the second part of the resolution, asking for it to be remitted to the NEC. The verdict of the conference, when the movers of the resolution refused to agree to this, went against him.

The 1970 conference then reflected a new mood which was not entirely confined to the Labour Party, a mood which demanded greater accountability, but also one of determination that the same mistakes must not be repeated by a future Labour government, and that party controls must be strengthened. This feeling was not to diminish over the years ahead; antipathy to the parliamentary leadership and MPs individually would increase in strength, especially after 1976. Other changes, however, were also taking place, which are relevant as a background to the main subject of this study, and which must be given a brief mention.

Changes within the trade unions meant that the block votes of the large unions were no longer automatically at the command of the leadership, The old right-wing block which had supported the parliamentary leadership much of the time since the war – the NUM and NUR for instance –

was shrinking, and newer, white-collar unions which did not share their traditional loyalist attitudes were growing in strength. The unions had become increasingly critical of the Wilson Government, and resentment over wage restraint had led to a new alignment within the union movement by 1970. Jones and Scanlon, heading the two largest unions, represented a powerful anti-elitist feeling, witness Jack Jones's remarks to the 1970 conference quoted above. He was now the leader of the Transport and General Workers, a union traditionally at the centre of the block of pro-leadership unions. Their loyalties, more than in the past, lay primarily with their own members. They recognised the need 'to move with the tide of industrial militancy and political leftism' (Minkin, 1978b, p. 343).

Changes were also to be seen on Labour's National Executive Committee. Its composition was always slow to reflect changes in the party, but in the last few years of the 1960s some new members on the left of the party had been elected to the committee in each of the three sections, unions, CLPs and women's section. These included Frank Allaun, Joan Lestor, Lena Jeger and Alex Kitson. The trend continued in the early 1970s, and by October 1974 the representation of the left on the committee was greater than that of the right. This development was chiefly the result of dissatisfaction with the leadership.

These two areas of change, within the unions and on the NEC, were also reflected in another change, this time in the party's staff. This was the appointment of Ron Hayward as Labour's National Agent in 1969 – described as 'an intentional interruption of 'Buggins' turn' (Butler and Pinto-Duschinsky, 1971, p. 53) – and subsequently in 1972 as General Secretary of the party. Hayward was a supporter of party democracy and welcomed the support of the left and of the trade unions. His duties when he became General Secretary were revealed specifically to include responsibility for 'propagating and seeking the implementation of the policies of the party as laid down by conference and the NEC'. He was also empowered to attend and speak at PLP meetings, and ensure parliamentary – NEC consultation. Already in 1970 the effects of these new alignments were making themselves felt in a variety of ways. One of these was in the politics of agenda management, which is exhaustively described in Minkin's book (1978b), and which could be interpreted very differently by different actors in the conference drama:

> Left-wing constituency Labour Party activists tended to see the whole process of agenda preparation as an orchestrated bureaucratic conspiracy in which a panoply of procedural, tactical and demagogic devices protected 'the platform' from the democratic will of the rank and file (p. 66).

On the other hand, the platform and the Conference Arrangements Committee did not have things all their own way; left-wingers often pushed themselves forward, to the embarassment of left-wing MPs who

> Sometimes went so far as to see the selection of delegates from the Trotskyist groups as part of an unholy alliance of the party's officials and its Marxist opponents to discredit the more moderate opposition by associating it with an extreme cause (p. 219).

By 1970, however, agenda controls were relaxed, in response to the 'new mood and power situation within the party' (p. 72, footnote 10). Political manipulation of the agenda became less marked than in the past and the chairmanship of the conference was more responsive to the wishes of the delegates.

In this new atmosphere it was possible for ideas about constitutional reform to surface and to be debated; not just the reselection of MPs, but the two other issues that were to become crucial over the ensuing decade, the election of the leader and the authorship of the manifesto, and other issues such as the election of the cabinet. But the NEC and the platform remained very much in control of what action was taken, and were indeed to a large extent protected by the 1968 decision that all proposals for amending the party constitution should first be remitted to the NEC for consideration and report back.

Two other changes mentioned in Chapter 1 may also be seen as a response to the general shift to the left which took place in the party after 1970, and here we may perhaps draw a parallel with the liberal whipping policy in the House of Commons after 1966, for they were all methods of dealing with dissent within the party. First, after some pressure, the list of proscribed organisations which dated back to 1924 was abolished, though groups that had their own separate aims, organisation and propaganda were to be repudiated. Secondly, the NEC tolerated the removal of MPs by constituency parties so long as the procedural rules, which had changed in 1970, were strictly adhered to. Neither of these changes fully satisfied the demand for more say for the rank and file in the running of the party. The fact that it became possible – though scarcely easy – for a constituency party to sack its MP did little to stem the demand for mandatory reselection a few years later.

The rise of that demand and the conference debates on the subject will be examined in detail in Chapters 7 and 8. But aside from the increasing strength of the left within the party, there was another issue which put into sharp focus the relationship of MPs to the rest of the party, and this was the question of British membership of the European Economic Community. At the time now being discussed, the early 1970s, this issue was closely linked with Labour attitudes to the Conservative government under Edward Heath. Supporting entry to the Common Market on the Tory terms became much less acceptable in a party which was more violently anti-Conservative than it had been for years.

Neil Kinnock's speech at the special Labour conference on the EEC held in July 1971 summed up this feeling dramatically. He said that the debate to be held in the Commons presented an opportunity to 'kick the Tories out of power', and went on,

> Even if it were the case that there were absolutely conclusive arguments, absolutely watertight arguments in favour of Europe ... if we want to maintain any kind of consistency at all, we cannot with one tongue be the enemies of this class-ridden government and with the other tongue embrace them and follow their policies.... And it is because I am a member of the Labour party, and because I am a trade unionist, and because I want to see the Tories beaten, and because I am willing to use any weapon to beat them, that I am against EEC entry on these terms at this time (Labour Party Annual Conference Report, 1971, p. 349).

The issue did not split the party evenly. Though most of the left were solidly against entry, anti-Marketeers were to be found in all sections and at all levels of the party. This, like Suez, was an issue which caught the imaginations of the activists. Though it had been decided to avoid an open split at the special conference in July by having no vote, the NEC had committed itself to presenting a resolution to the annual conference in October. For months the mainly right-wing, pro-Market MPs, led by Roy Jenkins, were subjected to enormous pressure from all quarters not to support the Heath Government and go against the views of a majority of the party.

The Jenkinsites were in an extremely difficult position, since they had to argue that the majority was wrong, which seemed to undermine the whole basis of their philosophy, as well as the unity of the party, and what is more 'played into the hands of those who called the liberals elitist' (Lazer, 1976, p. 273). Their intellectual arrogance irritated many who feared – justifiably in the short term at least – that they might get away with it.

The mood of the 1971 conference, when it met, was a noticeable and different one. If 1970 had been the year of participation and greater democracy, 1971 was the year when many delegates delivered their speeches beside the grave of consensus politics. 'Butskellism' was no longer acceptable to them. A. Evans MP was not the only one who detected this mood when he said

> This conference is now aware that the class war is a reality ... if there is one lesson that comes out of this Conference today, it is that consensus politics are dead, buried and unlamented (Labour Party Annual Conference Report 1971, p. 201).

Brian Sedgemore quoted Harry Truman with approval. 'If you have two Conservative parties, you can hardly blame the electorate for voting for the real thing.' This was not the kind of atmosphere in which Roy Jenkins and his followers would feel at ease; indeed they had been branded in advance as traitors by many on the left, who felt, as *Tribune* reported (8 October 1971) that 'the time was ripe for a little aggro'.[1] This feeling was not unanimous, however. Several Tribune MPs urged tolerance, and argued that the whip should not be withdrawn if the pro-Marketeers went against the party line.

The forthcoming House of Commons vote was a prominent issue at the conference. It had not yet been decided whether Labour MPs would be allowed a free vote, but the view was beginning to be widespread that if conference and the PLP could not control the pro-Marketeers, then their constituency parties might have to do so. Even Harold Wilson's speech calling for the whole parliamentary party to go into the lobbies against the Conservatives on 28 October made an oblique reference to this:

> There is not one Labour Member of Parliament who could have been elected by his own efforts. He is where he is because of the efforts of thousands upon thousands of those represented by delegates here today. And he is elected to be in his place and to do the job he was sent to do. (Labour Party Annual Conference Report 1971, p. 166.)

In spite of these words, it was widely suggested that Wilson was trying to shape a formula by which the pro-Marketeers would be allowed to vote for the principle of entry, provided they voted against the detailed legislation. This drew a furious reaction from Ian Mikardo, who echoed in blunter language Wilson's own speech. Such a deal, he said, would make Labour 'offensive to our friends and a welcome laughing-stock to our enemies . . . those sixty constituency parties will have the right, and some of them may exercise it, to pass a verdict on that shabby manoeuvre' (*The Times*, 7 October 1971). In addition, it was well known that the Lincoln Labour Party was preparing to replace Dick Taverne as their MP if he persisted in his pro-Market line, and a Socialist Charter bulletin on sale at the conference reminded constituency parties that 'it is possible for General Management Committees to reconsider their parliamentary representation if they become dissatisfied with their MP as a result of contravening a vital policy decision' (*The Times*, 9 October 1971). But mandatory reselection was not yet on the political agenda, even of any fringe group.

The conference voted five to one against EEC entry, but rejected a call for a referendum on the issue. As expected, this did not affect the Jenkins-

[1]Norman Atkinson was reported as saying 'All of us are wearing our bovver boots.'

ites and other pro-Marketeers, and in the Commons vote on 28 October, sixty-nine of them defied a three-line whip to vote with the Heath government in favour of British entry. The bitterness aroused by their action was long-lasting; they were regarded, and still are in some quarters, as the traitors who 'kept the Tories in power'. Their action increased suspicion of the parliamentary party as well as emphasising their distance from the majority of party members.[1] For the first time, many of the all-important centre of the PLP voted with the left.

The Common Market issue not only split the party deeply, but it raised once more fundamental questions about the role of an MP, opening up 'Labour's constitutional can of worms' (Lazer, 1976, p. 272), the notion that the PLP is not a sovereign body, and cannot vote against conference policy. Jenkins and his followers, all right-wingers, some of whom have never defied the whips before, were opposing not only their PLP colleagues but also an overwhelming conference vote. They justified their position – that the majority could be wrong – by citing appeasement and by invoking Burke. Indeed

> Burke's memorable definition of a representative's relation to his constituents hung like a cloud over the Labour benches throughout the debate (Lazer, 1976, p. 261).

Of the sixty-nine who voted for entry to the EEC, at least a dozen were retiring from the House at the next election; of the rest, a few had difficulties with their constituency parties, but Dick Taverne was the only one who was dismissed by his party. The whole episode was an important one for the Labour Party for a variety of reasons. For this analysis, what matters most is that it provoked still greater dissension between the parliamentary party and the CLPs, and that it was over this issue that for the first time the idea of 'reselection', later to become mandatory reselection, began to be common currency within the party. The case of Dick Taverne and the Lincoln Labour Party contributed decisively to the growing argument within the party on the role of its Members of Parliament.

---

[1]Subsequent events seem to have shown that some pro-Marketeers continued to give aid and comfort to the Conservatives during the passage of the detailed legislation for the European Communities Bill, by abstaining and thus easing the task of the government whips (Alan Watkins, *New Statesman* 23 June 1972 and 23 February 1973). No action was taken by the Labour whips. Many of the abstainers were retiring from the House at the next election, or their seats were due to disappear as a result of boundary changes. They were thus impervious to pressure from their constituencies.

6 The Taverne case and other disputes

The Taverne case is instructive for several reasons. It shows up the weaknesses of the Labour Party's selection procedure. It also demonstrates that the method then obtaining in the Labour Party for the dismissal of an MP was often long drawn out and uncertain of succeeding. Further, there was an extraordinary amount of interest shown by the mass media, both press and television. The later stages of Taverne's dispute with the Lincoln Labour Party were conducted under the spotlight of media attention, sometimes literally in the full glare of the television cameras. Finally the case exemplifies all the fundamental questions with which this study is concerned, about the position of the MP *vis-à-vis* his constituents, party activists, members and voters.[1]

When Taverne went into the Conservative lobby in October 1971, one of the sixty-nine MPs who defied the Whips, he was voting on a matter of principle which was important to him, for he had supported British entry to the EEC for years; but he also knew that he was putting in jeopardy his future as Lincoln's Labour MP.

A year later, on 6 October 1972, having been dismissed by his constituency party, and having lost an appeal to the National Executive Committee, he announced that he would resign and fight a by-election as an independent candidate. He gave a series of reasons for this. The first was the right of an MP to follow his conscience without being penalised for it. The second the neglect of Lincoln's problems by the Conservative government. Thirdly, he would campaign on the need for 'moderation' in industry. Fourth, he named the issue of whether the Lincoln Labour Party should be run 'by a caucus or by consultation'; and the last was to protest against the Labour Party's refusal to send representatives to the European Parliament, and its intention to renegotiate the terms of British entry to the Common Market.

This list summarises the points of disagreement between Taverne and

---

[1]Much of this chapter is based on Taverne's own account, supplemented by that in Cook and Ramsden (1973).

his CLP: the Common Market issue and that of legislation on industrial relations had been the chief policy matters on which they had found themselves at loggerheads in the previous few years. There had also been serious constitutional disagreements about how far an MP should be influenced by local party leaders, and about the running of the party, in particular, Taverne's objection to the growing left-wing element on the GMC. Finally, local problems and local politics had fed the ill-feeling which finally resulted in Taverne's dismissal.

Taverne had been selected in 1961 when the sitting MP, Geoffrey de Freitas (who later re-entered the House as MP for Kettering), was appointed High Commissioner to Ghana. This was at the height of Gaitskell's struggle with the left over unilateralism. Taverne was an active, even prominent, member of the Campaign for Democratic Socialism which successfully campaigned for the reversal of the 1960 decision of Labour's annual conference on unilateral disarmament. He had spoken in Gaitskell's defence at the 1959 annual conference,[1] soon after his speech proposing the amendment of Clause IV, the party's commitment to public ownership. At his selection conference, the tensions between Taverne and the local party, which were much later to come out into the open, were already present. Leo Beckett, a member of the GMC later to play a leading part in the dispute, walked out of the selection conference with three colleagues in protest at the similarity of views of the three nominees on the short list; as Taverne himself put it, it was 'politically a choice between Tweedledum, Tweedledee and their triplet brother'.[2] His record of the affair states that it was his membership of CDS which led Gaitskell to recommend him for the Lincoln seat: 'he was keen to see the leading younger figures of CDS brought into Parliament'. It was also thought that a man similar to de Freitas – both in legal background and 'moderate' views – was necessary, as the seat was vulnerable to the Conservatives, with a majority of 4400. But the small Gaitskellite majority on both the Executive Committee and the General Management Committee which had secured Taverne's selection was not to last, even till the by-election. Elections to the GMC soon swung the balance to the left, which was closely identified with the Campaign for Nuclear Disarmament.

Taverne was, therefore, as he wrote later, in a strange position from the moment of his adoption; the GMC was totally out of sympathy with his political views:

I was a Gaitskellite and Social Democratic MP who had been intro-

---

[1] He was parliamentary candidate for Putney at the time.
[2] The other two were Niall MacDermot and Arthur Bottomley (Taverne, 1974, p. 28).

duced to Lincoln because of the part I played in fighting the left-wing in CDS. I faced a GMC that was not just left-wing, but dominated by a small group of very determined left-wingers who knew what they were doing – fighting for power in the party, locally and nationally against people like myself (1974, p. 30).

Almost ten years were to elapse, however, before the CLP split under the strain of this incompatibility. Policy differences, as on nuclear disarmament, did arise, but there were also personal ones and it seems fairly clear that the question of class had a great deal to do with this. Tony Benn may not find his origins a handicap, but Taverne's Charterhouse and Balliol education, and his years at the bar, did nothing to endear him to the average working class party member. In spite of its cathedral and surrounding farmland, Lincoln is a city strongly dependent on engineering with 'the feel of an industrial town', and consequently with considerable AUEW strength in the local Labour Party.

Taverne saw his constituency difficulties as dating from the Labour general election victory of 1966. Disillusion with the Government began within a few months of the election; the unpopular decisions it took, or was forced into, were detailed in Chapter 4. In retrospect, Taverne was 'amazed how much active Labour party members tolerated'. The gradual disillusionment of the CLPs coincided with Taverne's promotion to ministerial office: he became a junior minister in the Home Office, then in April 1968 was moved to the Treasury, becoming Financial Secretary for the nine months preceding Labour's defeat in the 1970 general election. Having a job in the Government presented him with some conflicts of interest; he felt obliged to refuse to take part in a demonstration against the Wilson Government's economic policies, when as a result of 'shake-out' a factory in Lincoln was closed, with the loss of four hundred jobs. This caused some resentment. Even more bad feeling was aroused when prescription charges were reintroduced as part of the Government's post-devaluation cuts in January 1968, which came as a bitter blow to many on the Lincoln GMC. It was even suggested that Taverne should resign from the Government. *In Place of Strife* completed the disillusionment, but it was not until after the defeat of the government in the general election of June 1970, that the accumulated ill-feeling against Taverne really came into the open.

After 1970 the Labour Party shifted to the left, leaving many MPs in an exposed position. The issue which highlighted the differences between left and right in the party was that of Common Market entry, and this was also the case in Lincoln. But as with Nigel Nicolson and Suez, there was a previous disagreement which set the scene for the battle to follow. In the Nicolson case, the issue was capital punishment; with Taverne it was the highly contentious Conservative Industrial Relations Bill. It was on this subject that a serious argument between Taverne and his local party took place in January 1971, before a meeting of local shop stewards to discuss the bill. Taverne supported the Labour Party and TUC line at the time, which was that strike action should not be taken against the bill. But the CLP chairman, Don Gossop, who was also a local councillor and a shop steward at GEC in Lincoln and the new AUEW district secretary, favoured strike action. Also to be present at the meeting was Ernie Roberts, later to become Labour MP for Hackney, but at the time AUEW assistant secretary and a well-known militant. Before the meeting started, Taverne made it clear that he would strongly oppose any attempt to win support for strike action, and after a fierce argument succeeded in getting agreement that no such resolution would be forthcoming; but Gossop and three other leading members of the local party, including Taverne's agent Pat Mulligan, attacked Taverne for his 'middle class, legalistic and academic approach to politics'. Gossop went further, according to Taverne; he apparently said 'We will see that you are finished in Lincoln.' (1974, p. 54.)

Within a few months, the Common Market issue became a live one again, when the Heath Government succeeded in negotiating entry terms which were acceptable to them. Taverne already knew that his stand might pose serious problems for him in his constituency. From May 1971 until the Commons vote on 28 October, Taverne and his opponents became more and more firmly entrenched in their opposing positions, until it was clear that he was indeed finished, at least with the Lincoln Labour Party. It was in May that he made it clear to his agent that when the time came he would have to vote in favour of the terms which had been negotiated even if it meant voting against a three-line whip; the reply was 'Then you will have to take the consequences' (p. 56).

A specially organised GMC meeting on 2 July 1971, at which Taverne had invited John Silkin to put the anti-Market case, indicated a 'solid wall of opposition' to the Market, almost regardless of any terms. A few days later the GMC adopted a resolution for the special Labour conference on the EEC; this was strongly against entry and called on all MPs to oppose it. Taverne, although he writes in places with surprising sympathy for the disillusion of the left-wingers in the party, did not see this as an indication of the isolation from the rest of the party of the right-wing marketeers, but in purely personal terms: 'I suspect the resolution was directed at me as much as at the Party Conference. Either it was a warning or it was designed to put me on the spot' (p. 57). In the event, no vote was taken at the special conference on 17 July but *at Taverne's request* another special GMC meeting was held, to discuss the relations between an MP and his constituency party. He felt this went well, although he relates that he was subjected to a strong attack on two grounds: first that the conscience clause for MPs who failed to vote with their party did not apply to major policy issues, but only to those where moral or religious scruples might be involved; and secondly, that 'one could really not disregard the majority view of both the local party and the full Labour Party Conference'. These were, he says, to become 'a familiar chorus' later on, and adds: 'At later meetings they could cite the majority view of the Parliamentary Labour Party as well' (p. 59).

By the time the annual Labour Conference took place early in October, it was well-known that some Labour pro-Marketeers would vote in favour of entry. Conference voted against by five to one, and there was a rising tide of ill-feeling against those who were prepared to support the Heath government. This was accompanied by increasing speculation in the press about the difficulties that the pro-Market MPs would face in their constituencies. Taverne was the chief focus of such speculation; an item in the Diary column of *The Times* on the subject mentioned by name only Taverne and indeed quoted Leo Beckett, Lincoln's conference delegate, as expressing the hope that if Taverne voted in the Conservative lobby a resolution of no confidence in him would be passed by the GMC.

So Lincoln was already a centre of attention for the media; then only a few days before the Commons vote on October 28, Granada TV broadcast a *World in Action* programme ostensibly dealing with the broad issues of relations between an MP and his local party, but in fact devoting all its time to the dispute at Lincoln. It seems to have aroused enormous bitterness in the city: a 'slanging match' between Taverne and his critics took place and the general atmosphere grew less conducive to any sort of compromise. Pat Mulligan's last minute plea to Dick Taverne on 28 October, 'for God's sake abstain', fell on deaf ears and he voted with the Conservative government.

Immediately after the Commons vote, Lincoln CLP moved to oust Taverne. The first GMC meeting, for technical reasons,[1] was unable to pass a resolution that Taverne should retire at the next general election. A fortnight later, such a resolution *was* passed by a close margin (55–51, with five abstentions), but before the necessary second meeting took place, some Taverne supporters mounted a 'counter-revolution'. They succeeded in passing an Executive Committee resolution that no further action should be taken, and the subsequent GMC meeting, in a vote on this, tied 45–45 – it was stalemate.

In the ensuing hiatus, Taverne, surprisingly and, as he later admitted, inconsistently, offered to vote against the detailed Common Market legislation. Some of his opponents, he wrote were 'mollified' by this belated attempt at compromise and there was a move, well-intentioned perhaps,

[1]The 1970 party rules that two separate GMC meetings, four weeks apart, had to pass a retirement resolution, with the agenda being circulated in advance.

but not well thought out, to suggest to Transport House that he should be found another seat. Early in 1972, the anti-Taverne faction further increased their strength on the GMC, but no action against him was initiated immediately, perhaps because of imminent local elections.

Taverne, temporarily saved, knew that 'one further step out of line would almost certainly mean compulsory retirement' (p. 70). This step he took in mid-April, when he resigned from the opposition front bench, where he had been economic spokesman, seconding Roy Jenkins, who also resigned. This was a protest against the shadow cabinet's support for a proposed referendum on the Common Market. Anti-Marketeers in Lincoln 'saw this as the ultimate act in Taverne's apparent determination to flout party unity' (Ramsden and Jay in Cook and Ramsden (eds.), 1973, p. 276). Once again, the GMC moved to sack their MP: two meetings on 10 May and 19 June 1972, voted that he should retire at the next election. In the interval between the two, however, Taverne made a public and highly publicised attempt to prove to his opponents that the ordinary voters of Lincoln supported him. He did this by commissioning an opinion poll. Its results were published a few days before the second GMC meeting. They showed strong support for Taverne as Lincoln's MP, and for his action on the Common Market issue. Having been duly voted out by the GMC on 19 June,[1] Taverne decided to appeal to the NEC. The purpose of the prescribed four-week interval between GMC meetings in such cases, he contended, was to allow consultation to take place in the various wards which make up a constituency. Not only was this not done, he alleged, it was deliberately frustrated.

This appeal was allowed by the special committee of enquiry set up by the NEC's organisation sub-committee, and by the sub-committee itself, but rejected by the full NEC. The chairman, Tony Benn, later told the PLP that although the failure to consult constituted a breach of natural justice, the letter of the party constitution had been adhered to: it did not explicitly lay down that the interval between the two obligatory GMC meetings should be used for consultation with ward committees. Taverne, not unnaturally, depicts Benn as the villain of the piece, claiming that he initially tried to prevent any hearing of the appeal, and when the NEC did consider the reports from the two sub-committees, he delayed discussion of the matter so long that at least two potential Taverne supporters had departed. Certainly, Benn made not one but two speeches hostile to Taverne and when the Committee voted 12–8 against Taverne, it seemed to split into left and right-wing factions.

John Chalmers of the Boilermakers' Union and chairman both of the

---

[1] Taverne (1974) indicates that the meeting was a formality: Ramsden and Jay say it was stormy.

organisation sub-committee and the enquiry committee, who had apparently supported Taverne's appeal, later wrote an article for *Tribune* in which he defended the dismissal, concluding 'Politics is not for simple, honest men: it is for those who seek power' (*Tribune*, 13 October 1972). Taverne, of course, was no more a simple man than his Lincoln opponents, and by the time this article appeared, his resignation as MP and his intention to fight a by-election had been announced.

Taverne's written submission to the NEC at the time of his appeal included these words:

> I fully accept that I am accountable to local Party Members as a whole for my general conduct as Member of Parliament. It would, however, I suggest, be wrong to allow a local party to dismiss its Member because of one single vote (p. 168).

But although the question of voting in the House was much discussed, it is quite clear that his dismissal, as so often in such cases, came as the culmination of a series of disputes and disagreements, and that a certain animosity had existed ever since Taverne's adoption in 1961. Taverne himself was quite aware of this; indeed the quotation on p. 7 above shows that he and many of the local activists regarded each other with suspicion right from the start. A *New Statesman* comment on the *World in Action* programme is worth quoting. 'What kept coming through', it said, 'was the memory of the Lincoln Party's resentment at having Taverne foisted on them in the first place' (*New Statesman* Diary, 29 October 1971). An 'undercurrent of resentment' (James Fenton, *New Statesman*, 23 June 1972) certainly seems to have existed and though the differences between Taverne and some of the Lincoln party were clearly and obviously political, there were also personal ones.

Taverne was an intellectual, and not a good mixer; he also limited his contacts with the active party workers. In addition, he seemed very sensitive, especially on the question of class. One of the most wounding, and most resented, charges made by Leo Beckett on the *World in Action* programme was that Taverne was 'ill at ease with the working man' (p. 77). There was obviously some truth in this; a notably sympathetic article in *The Times*, which was strongly partisan on Taverne's behalf throughout the affair, said that his inability to mix easily made him seem more arrogant than he really was, adding that he was 'too much of an intellectual to be fully appreciated by some members of his own party'. This arrogance shows through, even where Taverne is admitting his own faults: 'I feel now in retrospect that I might have made a more determined effort to keep on good terms with the people whose views I profoundly disagreed with.' Taverne himself noticed a growing feeling of class resentment in Lincoln; and to some commentators at least, the most striking characteristic of

Grafton House, the Lincoln Labour Party headquarters, was its working-class membership, not its left-wing tendencies. Many of these people regarded Taverne with deep suspicion by the time he resigned, and in spite of Taverne's denials, class probably had a good deal to do with this.

Personal feelings apart, Taverne and many of the active members of the local party disagreed on a wide range of political issues. Though he can at times write with sympathy about the feelings of the left towards the Wilson Government, his views could hardly have been more different; indeed he seems to have been strongly opposed to the left-wing of the party, as the following quotation shows:

> The political sympathies of the GMC can best be shown by referring to the lists of guests invited to annual dinners (etc.) . . . they read like a roll-call of the leading figures from the Tribune Group . . . [Atkinson, Mikardo and Mendelson are named]. One of my right-wing friends complained after one May Day meeting at Grafton House that it was more like a Communist party than a Labour party rally (p. 45).

The most striking thing about this disparity between the views of the MP and those of his local party is that the selection ever took place; Taverne was clearly not, to use his own phrase 'a suitable horse for the Lincoln course'. His politics and his personality made him an unsuitable match for the local party, and highlight once again the fact that the selection system leaves a great deal to be desired. But there were several other factors at work relevant to the dispute.

The first of these is the change, touched on in Chapter 5, that was taking place in the Labour Party in the late 1960s and early 1970s. For many in the Labour Party, consensus politics was a thing of the past, but the leftward shift seems not to have had much impact on Taverne. In these changing political conditions, the right wing of the parliamentary party was losing touch with the rest of the party, a state of affairs highlighted by the Common Market issue. Taverne, of course, was only one of many Labour MPs who were prepared to vote for the entry terms, but he was a 'militant' rather than a 'pacifier' on the issue (Alan Watkins, *New Statesman*, 4 August 1972). This 'militancy' was indicated in his contribution to the first debate on the terms of entry, when Geoffrey Rippon presented his proposals to the House of Commons. His remarks seemed intended to irritate rather than contribute to the debate. He asked if Rippon was aware that 'most of those who genuinely wanted the negotiations to succeed will regard the outcome as satisfactory and acceptable – this is, as opposed to those who did not wish them to succeed?' (Hansard, Parliamentary Debates 5th Series, Commons 1970/71, vol. 819, col. 1622).

Taverne's sticking point, then, was the Common Market, rather as

Nicolson's had been Suez. Later, as we have seen, he went further and resigned from the opposition front bench on the referendum question. But, as with the Nicolson case, Taverne was not the only member who followed a line which ran counter to most of the rest of his party. He was, however, the only one to be dismissed by his local party: Nicolson was one of several, the rest of whom went quietly. Some of the sixty-eight Labour Members who went with Taverne into the Conservative lobby in October 1971 did have difficulties with their local parties; Edward Lyons, MP for Bradford West, survived a call for his retirement by a vote of 35–20, and William Rodgers, an old CDS man like Taverne and a close friend and colleague, survived fairly easily, it seems. Diarist for *Socialist Commentary* at the time, Rodgers recorded that his own GMC was fair. After some criticism, it expressed 'respect for my opinions and confidence in me as Stockton's Member of Parliament' (*Socialist Commentary*, December 1971). David Marquand, another Jenkinsite and pro-Marketeer, suffered what seems to have been an altogether stormier meeting at Ashfield; he had apparently escaped Taverne's fate by the skin of his teeth, and only on the promise that he would never vote in a Tory Lobby again (see a letter to *Socialist Commentary*, March 1972, p. 25). All of these people are now members of the Social Democratic Party. Some Conservative MPs, too, suffered severe problems in their constituencies as a result of taking an anti-EEC line, but none lost his seat.

What then distinguished Taverne from the rest? As with Nicolson, the difference is that he was determined to fight, determined not to compromise. The result of this, as in the Nicolson case, is that the party turned against him, though individual MPs may have taken a different view. Given the mixture of politics and personalities involved, there is a sense in which the conflict and Taverne's dismissal were inevitable. He himself admits as much; he confessed to being argumentative and as the dispute dragged on, he gradually came round to the point of view that a 'showdown' would be preferable to other alternatives – 'relations with the officers had become impossible and were clearly past repair' (p. 70). As early as 1971, before his House of Commons vote, Taverne seemed completely intransigent. Leo Beckett was quoted as saying that the CLP were seeking a compromise with Taverne; 'We have leant over backwards over the years to try and help him ... but he doesn't seem to want [to get] off the hook' (*The Times*, Diary, 7 October 1971). By his refusal to countenance the use of the Common Market issue to defeat the government, and his determination that the local party could have no say on his stand in Parliament, Taverne made sure that dismissal was the only outcome.

There were some half-hearted attempts at reconciliation but these were doomed to failure in view of Taverne's determination not to compromise with the left wing in Lincoln: he had made the decision to stand as an independent candidate, but postponed resignation to appeal to the NEC on the question of irregularities in some wards. While the appeal was in progress and a verdict favourable to him still seemed possible, he viewed such an outcome with mixed feelings, so strongly did he now favour the resignation option. Taverne, then, was determined to fight, even to be martyred for his cause if necessary. Such a prospect was viewed with alarm by most of the rest of the party – leadership and PLP alike.

By October 1972, when Taverne announced his resignation, the party was beginning to heal the wounds caused the previous year by the EEC vote. The conference, which was just ending when Taverne made his announcement, had passed a Common Market resolution which, by avoiding both extremes, succeeded in giving comfort to both sides of the argument. An election in the spring of 1973 was a possibility, and relations between pro-Market MPs and their CLPs were being patched up. In these circumstances Taverne's decision seemed designed to threaten the fragile unity of the party and those on the right of the NEC felt isolated without going out of their way to defend Taverne. Individual MPs whose constituency party relations were improving had no wish to see an upheaval of the kind which Taverne sought. *Tribune* (11 August 1972) reported that MPs, such as Roy Hattersley, on the pro-Market wing of the party just wished Taverne would 'silently fade away'. Taverne sensed a coolness among his parliamentary friends, who feared that the influence of the Jenkinsites would be weakened; 'All of them would be tainted by my dis- loyalty' (p. 86). And there was certainly a strong feeling, even on the right, that Taverne had committed a breach of trust. Brian Walden said: 'Of course an MP must have strong opinions of his own, and I have defied the Labour Party Whip more than Dick Taverne has. We owe the Labour Party an unpayable debt and Dick has ratted on a lifetime of obligation.' (*The Times*, 9 October 1972, quoted from the television programme 'Weekend World'.) Callaghan was alleged to have said: 'We must execute Taverne.' (Ramsden and Jay, in Cook and Ramsden (eds.), 1973, p. 281 and *Spectator*, 13 January 1973.) It is worth noting, however, that in the ensuing by-election campaign, none of the Jenkinsites spoke on behalf of Dilks, the official Labour candidate in Lincoln. Roy Hattersley was said to have explained this with an analogy which echoed Callaghan's remark, but which the result would show was false: it was not customary for the desert- er's friends to form the firing squad.

Taverne's NEC appeal, as we saw, argued that an MP should not be dismissed on the strength of one vote against the party in the Commons, and the case did give rise to a debate on the conscience clause. Could it protect him from dismissal? This had been a major part in the argument against him in Lincoln – had he merely abstained, it was said, accommodation would have been possible, and this point was also raised during the NEC's consideration of his appeal.

Left-wing MPs, who had often been in trouble with the Whips for voting against the Labour Government of 1966–70, joined in the argument: their votes, they said, had been in line with Conference decisions, and the Tribune Group prided themselves on the fact that they never went into the lobby with the Conservatives.

What was more, as another left-winger, Stan Newens, argued in a letter to *The Times* (13 October 1972), they were frequently backed not only by the decisions of the annual conference, but also by their CLPs. Taverne seemed to be refusing to acknowledge the need to take account of the views of anyone at all on the EEC issue.

A powerful contribution to this debate was made by Richard Crossman in an article in *The Times* immediately after Taverne's unsuccessful appeal. He argued that the liberal whipping regime introduced by Silkin and himself in the 1960s – of which Taverne and his sixty-eight fellow-Marketeers had been the beneficiaries as much as any of the Tribunites – meant that the 'only check on our [i.e. MPs'] behaviour is that which our constituency parties exert' (*The Times*, 2 August 1972).

Crossman mentioned several Conservative MPs who had had difficulties with their local associations as a result of their anti-Market views, in which they could expect no help from Conservative Party head-quarters. He argued that the right to defy the party line in the House had a correlative responsibility: that of fighting one's own battle in the constit-uency. While clearly written to justify the NEC's decision in the Taverne case, this argument is a powerful one. An MP must be subject to some control, if not in the House, then elsewhere. Interestingly, the idea that discipline might be exerted more through the constituency party than the Whip's Office has a tradition in the Conservative Party. Crossman's ideas on discipline, as we saw elsewhere, owed much to how things were done in the Conservative Party. And although many differences may be pointed out between the Nicolson and Taverne cases, the last word in both cases was allowed to the local party. A Labour MP has greater constraints to deal with, being a member of a party which is much more strongly committed to a set of basic principles and to a programme. One verdict on the Taverne case gave this great emphasis:

> Labour MPs remain delegates of a party with whose principles and programme they are in general accord. Flexibility and compromise is required both by the MPs and the constituency parties. (Seyd, 1974, p. 246.)

The Taverne case had a deep effect on the Labour Party. It emphasised the divisions in the party between the right-wing MPs and left-wing activists, between activists and ordinary voters. The dismissal of Taverne's appeal by the NEC indicated the increased strength of the left of the party on that committee. The episode also strengthened the feeling on the left of the party that CLPs should more easily be able to dismiss their MPs and was an important contributing factor in the foundation of the Campaign for Labour Party Democracy.

It was in response to the new mood within the party which favoured greater accountability, and also as a riposte to Taverne and other MPs who had voted in favour of EEC entry, that the Tribune group of MPs published a pamphlet in July 1972 in time to have an impact on resolutions then being formulated for the annual conference, and indeed at about the time that Taverne's appeal was being heard.

The authors of this pamphlet, entitled *Labour – Party or Puppet?* were three members of the Tribune group, Frank Allaun, Ian Mikardo and Jim Sillars. The broad argument that it contained, that the democratic system of the party was not functioning properly, was endorsed by the forty-two members of the group. They subscribed to the view that there should be greater participation by ordinary party workers.

> We cannot win and hold party workers by expecting them to be mute cogs in an electoral machine . . . we cannot expect them to continue their efforts in support of a programme which they have never had a hand in formulating, and for which their approval was never sought (p. 4).

When the wishes of the activists are ignored, the consequences are disastrous: and under the Wilson Government of 1964–70, 'life in Labour's strictly limited democracy became intolerable for many party members' (p. 4), hence the decline in membership and activity. Concern was expressed about the gap, which had become more pronounced, between the ordinary members and the party elite, mainly consisting of MPs. Various reforms were proposed to deal with these defects: changing the representation on the NEC, which would be empowered to review government actions, the election of the party leader by the whole conference, and several proposals to improve both the selection and accountability of MPs.

Selection procedures, the pamphlet argued, were too sketchy and favoured the professional rather than the working-class candidate, putting a premium on 'charm and on smooth, articulate performance' (p. 7). This aspect of selection should be improved by greater availability of information on candidates and their views, and a more thorough selection process generally. Much more controversially, it was also proposed that the selection conference, instead of consisting of the entire General Management Committee, should include only those who attended meetings regularly, in order to prevent the regular activists finding themselves with a candidate they did not want.

Turning to the question of accountability of MPs to conference, the pamphlet suggested that they should sign an undertaking to stand by the 'programme and policy of the party as decided by conference'. In addition, to 'assist in getting the parliamentary party closer to the party' (p. 15), the PLP's standing orders should also be approved by conference. Declaring that the maxims of Burke were not fitted for a modern democracy, the pamphlet thus argued for a return to the situation before 1906, when the party's representation in Parliament was miniscule and before Labour had decided to set up as a national party.

The ideas set out in this small pamphlet contained most of the radical constitutional reforms which were to be pressed by the left at successive conferences during the 1970s, though it did not include the idea of automatic reselection. They immediately found powerful critics. These included Douglas Houghton, a former PLP chairman, who declared that if implemented they would make Labour 'unfit to govern', and John Mackintosh, a prominent right-winger and academic. Both based their objection to the proposals on the fact that voting in conference was dominated by the block votes of the large trade unions, whose influence was enlarged as individual party membership fell.

Resolutions submitted to the 1972 Annual Conference echoed the Tribune line, and some went further. A series of resolutions on the proper relationship between MPs and conference was remitted to the NEC. One composite resolution proposed that the PLP should insist that all Labour MPs abide by conference decisions, and condemned Members acting in opposition to the 'declared majority decisions of the party'. Such MPs, said the resolution, should resign 'or not be endorsed again' (Labour Party Annual Conference Report, 1973, pp. 14–16). The NEC's answer in its report the following year was that this was a matter for local parties and the PLP. This attitude on the part of the NEC was made even clearer in its reply to another remitted resolution, which demanded that 'elected representatives should be made accountable to their appropriate management body'. The NEC reply was as follows:

> The NEC supports the view that delegates are responsible to the party units which appoint them and that Members of Parliament ... are answerable to the local parties responsible for their selection. (Labour Party Annual Conference Report 1973, pp. 14–16.)

A third resolution went further still. Deploring the excessive freedom allowed to the parliamentary party, it urged, among other reforms, improved selection procedures including a reselection conference after ten years, and depriving the NEC of its power to alter constituency decisions about candidates.[1] The NEC declined to accept all of this, but referred some (unspecified) parts to the area consultations on party structure which took place in 1973, and which were debated at the 1974 Annual Conference.

Similarly, in 1973, several resolutions that appeared on the conference agenda proposed greater accountability and reselection after ten years. 'Members of Parliament', read one, 'should have reasonable freedom of action, but a Labour Member should not be regarded as selected for life.' A local Labour Party should be able to decide that the MP no longer held their confidence, it continued. This was likely to be rare, but at the same time to cause antagonism, and it therefore proposed a reselection conference after ten years, with the MP on the shortlist as a matter of right. This, like all resolutions proposing constitutional amendments, was remitted to the NEC for discussion at the next year's conference.

The proposal probably fairly accurately reflected the feeling in the party at the time. While there were a number of MPs involved in longstanding disputes with their local parties, and doubtless others where the activists were dissatisfied with the MP, at this stage there was no concerted campaign for mandatory reselection, rather a feeling that it should be easier to get rid of an unsatisfactory MP.

In most constituencies, however, this was still far from easy. Several well-publicised disputes dragged on for years. The infinitely complex Prentice case which ended in a welter of legal writs and injunctions, and the imposition of a candidate for the 1979 election by the NEC had its beginnings in the early 1970s.[1] The moribund Newham North East party, most of whose members were past retiring age, was 'taken over' by dint of hard work by young left-wingers moving into the constituency. Their first attempt to win a no confidence vote against Prentice took place in December 1973. This was defeated by two to one, and the moves against Prentice were not renewed until 1975, when they were successful. There then followed a prolonged battle between the moderate and extreme factions in the CLP. But Prentice, who provided the leadership with one of its most embarrassing moments when he joined the Conservative party in October 1977, had been troublesome since 1973 when he made a speech calling for the 'moderates' in the party to stand up and be counted. As his later career made plain, his natural home was not the Labour Party; and although what took place in Newham was unpleasant it was certainly not repeated elsewhere. It is at least possible, even likely, that someone such as

[1]For text of all these, see Labour Party Conference Report 1973, pp. 14–16. The sources of these resolutions are not given.
[2]An account of the Prentice affair, from the 'moderate' point of view, has been given by the Oxford student who 'counter-infiltrated' the Newham NE party (see McCormick, 1979).

Prentice, perfunctory about constituency matters and increasingly at odds with the trend in the party on policy, might have faced a challenge to his continuing as the MP in any case.

An associate of Prentice's was another London MP, Frank Tomney. He was the only MP who was actually prevented by his local party from standing at the 1979 general election, but the dispute had been continuing intermittently for years before that. He was one of the few Labour MPs who truly merited the description 'extreme moderate' and his association with Prentice did him no good. But he had earned the hatred of the left in the constituency, Hammersmith North, long before when he stood against the previous MP, D. N. Pritt in 1950. Pritt had represented the seat since 1935, but had been expelled from the party in 1940 because of his support for the Russian invasion of Finland. The antagonism between Tomney and some in the local party was therefore longstanding, but he had been successful in resisting several attempts to dismiss him. He had always opposed radical reform, being the only Labour MP to vote for the retention of capital punishment in 1965; he had also favoured EEC entry and supported American policy in Vietnam, but had been backed by the left in the constituency against Ivor Richard when he was reselected following the amalgamation of Hammersmith North and Barons Court constituencies in 1971 as a result of boundary changes. Immediately following the October 1974 election, he was asked to resign at the end of the parliament; Tomney was already 65, and a move to dismiss him had lapsed because of the election. He was finally rejected by his CLP in February 1976, and his appeal to the NEC in July confirmed that decision. Tomney bitterly attacked this ruling, alleging corrupt practice and condemning the fact that there was 'nothing for loyalty, nothing for principle, nothing for dedication'.

Liverpool as well as London was the scene for such disputes. Two MPs found themselves in difficulties with their constituency parties, and again both were disputes which had been going on for some time. The first, Sir Arthur Irvine, a barrister, had been the subject of several dismissal attempts. The chief reason for this seems to have been neglect of constituency duties. In 1971 the NEC had overruled the constituency party, but they finally voted him out in May 1977. His death intervened, however, and the consequent by-election was a fascinating curtain-raiser to the 1979 general election. On the day Callaghan announced the general election, the young Liberal candidate, David Alton, won a striking victory, based largely on a very active and prolonged devotion to 'community politics' by the local Liberal Party.

Elsewhere in Liverpool, Richard Crawshaw, Member for Toxteth from 1964, also faced problems. The Militant Tendency was gaining ground in Toxteth as in other local constituencies, but his unpopularity dated back to his early days in the House when he advocated the use of force after the Rhodesian UDI. The left in the constituency disliked his firm support for the Labour Government's unpopular economic policies, and the substantial Catholic vote could not have approved his firm stand in favour of abortion. He also sponsored Dick Taverne on his re-entry to the House after the Lincoln by-election in 1973. Attempts to dismiss Crawshaw had come to nothing when he joined the Social Democratic Party in 1981.

These and other disputes dragged on, lending weight to the views of those who thought that dismissal should be easier. At the same time, the divisions in the party were becoming more noticeable. With Prentice and Benn both making speeches attacking the opposing wing of the party, Wilson himself rebuked 'extremists' on both wings of the party in December 1973. Organised factions within the party were proliferating and it was an indication of the gulf between Westminster and the constituencies that these tended to be either exclusively parliamentary and weak in the rest of the country, such as the Tribune Group and the Manifesto Group, which was founded in December 1974, or non-parliamentary such as the Social Democratic Alliance, also founded in 1974.

After two general elections in 1974, the party was now returned to government with the dangerously small majority of three and was in effect dependent on Liberal support from 1975, though there was no formal pact until 1977. As in 1966–70, parliamentary discipline was a problem. In the seven major revolts that took place between October 1974 and February 1976, almost half of the rebels were new MPs. The harassed chief whip, Robert Mellish was quoted as saying, only two months after the election: 'All constituency parties should now see their MPs – and particularly new MPs – so as to tell them what party they actually belong to.' (*The Times*, 27 December 1974.) And as before, the left grew increasingly dissatisfied with the Government's performance and especially with its economic policies. Wage restraint from mid-1975, and the watering down of the Industry Bill after the demotion of Benn, added injury to the insult of the left's defeat in the June 1975 referendum on the EEC. The sterling crises of 1976, culminating in severe deflation imposed by the IMF, accompanied by rising unemployment, all contributed to the unpopularity of the leadership both in the CLPs and on the left of the parliamentary party.

In these circumstances, the Campaign for Labour Party Democracy made continuous progress in its fight for mandatory reselection. By means of model resolutions, the CLPD carefully orchestrated a campaign which was favoured not only by extreme left-wingers, but across a broad spectrum of the party. And at the 1974 party conference the issue was first properly debated. However, before examining developments at the 1974 conference it is worth considering the case of Eddie Griffiths, who was ousted just three months before that conference took place.

7 The case of Eddie Griffiths and Sheffield Brightside

The Griffiths case stands in contrast to most of the other disputes that have been mentioned. It was remarkable for the speed with which the local party succeeded in dismissing the MP. It attracted little attention at the time, except locally, and has not previously been studied in detail. What follows is based largely on interviews with those involved and on the Brightside party records which they made available, but the principal actor, Griffiths himself, has remained silent.

The case marked a turning point in the lead-up to the reselection campaign proper. It foreshadowed the importance of issues that have subsequently been fiercely argued in the party, particularly about the power which activists have over their MP. Should they have the right to dismiss him if they so wish, without recourse to the rest of the party, or to the electorate as a whole? The central issue between Griffiths and his party was not how far he should follow instructions, or indeed about his voting record in the House of Commons, but the fact that there arose between the MP and the leaders of the local party strong feelings of mutual antipathy. These were based partly on differences about personal behaviour which both sides took care to downplay. But there were also political differences, which reflected the changes that were taking place in the Labour Party and which emphasised the divide between an MP at Westminster and active members at the grassroots. Griffiths said that his real fault was that he was, 'too loyal to the Labour Party'; the leaders of the Brightside party felt that he was out of touch with their sort of Labour politics. Several of their specific complaints against him concerned his failure to take part in direct action on issues which they felt to be important and with which he would not associate himself; but these were fairly minor, and in many ways there was no real dispute, rather a determination by a small group to get rid of an MP with whom they no longer had any sympathy, political or personal.

The case also shows up once again the inadequacies of the selection procedure. As at Lincoln, the Brightside party found that they had not got a like-minded MP. To the extent that that was the root of the matter, problems were bound to arise, but the story which follows also shows how difficult it is for an MP to satisfy his local party. Griffiths failed to satisfy them on any of the four criteria discussed in Chapter 3. His status in the parliamentary party was not high, his political beliefs were out of tune with those of his General Management Committee, and his contribution to constituency life and his social relationships with the local party also failed to come up to the minimum standard.

As with Taverne, local politics played an important part in the background to the dispute. What had happened at Lincoln had a strong influence on the local party leaders in Brightside; their self-discipline in revealing nothing to the mass media was a reaction against what thay had seen during the Taverne affair. But there are more contrasts than similarities between the two cases. There was no fertile ground for the social democrats to cultivate in Brightside. The constituency is a thoroughly working-class one, in what has been described as the most working-class city in Europe. The majority of the electorate are council tenants, living in huge pre-war estates and working in the steel and engineering factories on the eastern edge of the constituency. Trade unionism is, therefore, a strong tradition, and it is to the AUEW that many naturally belong. But this is probably a less strong influence than the social cohesion for which Brightside is exceptional, even in a city with an unusually stable population and a strong sense of community. Local ties of work and friendship played an important part in the local Labour Party.

Naturally enough, the Brightside seat is solidly Labour. Up to 1968 only two MPs had represented it in Parliament since 1935. Fred Marshall was MP from 1935 to 1950, and then Dick Winterbottom from 1950 until his death in February 1968. He had followed the tradition established by Marshall of living in the city and keeping in close touch with his constituents. But – and this was also in keeping with the tradition of politics in Sheffield – he was not, although he moved to the city after his election, a local man, nor was the union which sponsored him – USDAW – closely connected with the industrial life of the city. This was also quite normal:

> In the industrial constituencies of Sheffield the Labour Party members wanted a trade-union sponsored candidate, but within this constraint their choice depended on the policies and personalities of the rival applicants, and not upon the particular union to which he might belong. (Hampton, 1970, p. 79.)

Winterbottom was not a distinguished parliamentarian, but he was a good constituency MP. Most of those interviewed mention this unasked. He lived in the constituency and was known to all: 'You could go and knock on his door any time.' He never held surgeries but 'pursued a vigorous and highly personal "open door policy" ' (Hampton, 1970, p.

206). He made a monthly report to the local party, and keenly supported local causes, for example clean-air legislation. His obituary described him as 'a man of the people' (Sheffield *Morning Telegraph*, 12 February 1968); as such he suited the constituency admirably. One of his greatest assets, apart from this, was his excellent agent. Again, most of those interviewed expressed the opinion that had Griffiths had the same agent, things would never have turned out as they did. Winterbottom's majority never fell below 16,000 but when he died the signs of change within the Labour Party – and indeed in British politics as a whole – were already beginning to be seen.

Locally, Labour Party politics in Sheffield were in turmoil, chiefly on account of a scheme which would increase council rents and give rebates to some tenants. The main burden of the increases was to fall on the tenants in the older estates, of the type which made up the Brightside constituency. The scheme was opposed by most tenants and seriously split the Labour Party in the city. In response to the plan, tenants' associations sprang up. These, partly financed by the AUEW, and run by people with no previous political experience – an 'alliance of housewives and Trotskyist intellectuals' was how one writer described them – rapidly became a major political force, though their rent strike quickly petered out. Opposition to the rent increases, and the unpopularity of the Wilson Government, allowed the Conservatives to take control of the City Council in the May 1968 elections for the first time since 1932. Many who normally voted Labour had stayed at home or voted for Communist candidates.

This episode illustrated the strength of feeling which could be aroused in a usually apathetic electorate over an issue which closely affected them. Although the middle class takeover of local Labour parties discerned in Liverpool at this period by Hindess (1971) could not be said to be in any way true of Brightside then or later, some of his *aperçus* are relevant to the case. The tenants' associations – widely perceived to be 'non-political' – did provide an alternative to apathy for those who had drifted away from Labour, and gave support to his contention that politics as conducted by the Labour establishment did not meet the political needs of many of the working class (Hindess, 1971). The affair shook the Labour Party badly and showed how the local Labour establishment could be threatened by a combination of 'non-political' tenants, Communists, and opposition from within their own ranks:

> The Party realised more closely that it needed to fight for local working-class support, that it could not expect the local Labour movement to go on supporting it just because it was the Labour Party.

The experiences of 1967 and 1968 and the radicalisation of some who were previously apolitical had a direct influence on subsequent events in Brightside. One of the leaders of the tenants' movement was later active against Griffiths. Later still he joined the Liberal Party.

Nationally, too, the spring of 1968 was a bleak time for the Labour Party. From July 1966 to November 1967, Labour had lost six out of nine seats in the worst series of by-election defeats in British political history. As one analyst described it:

> a pattern was emerging: party workers reluctant to work, disillusioned not only by the government's economic record but also in many cases by its behaviour over defence and Vietnam; and voters who saw no reason to turn out for a party which in their view had brought down upon them a cruel collection of miseries. (D. McKie in Cook and Ramsden, 1973, p. 249.)

The winter months of 1967–68 brought worse. The EEC veto, devaluation, public spending cuts, the reintroduction of prescription charges, all damaged the government's standing still further. Winterbottom's death brought the number of by-elections pending to eight. Roy Jenkins's savage Budget on 19 March 1968 was soon followed by three crucial by-elections at Dudley, Acton and Meriden on 28 March. Labour lost them all on huge pro-Conservative swings, and six weeks later gained only 450 seats in nationwide municipal elections.

Small wonder then that even an election in a normally safe seat such as Brightside worried the party. Locally, at least, a lot of interest was aroused in the by-election. The selection process followed a normal pattern. The fourteen initial nominations included two local councillors, two former MPs and five future MPs.[1] And Eddie Griffiths.

The short list held five names. It has been suggested that Griffiths was only included to make up numbers; his union,[2] though fairly well represented, did not normally use its votes very energetically on such occasions. He had just been made one of the first worker-directors of the British Steel Corporation, and though he would have to resign this post on being elected to Parliament, it may have been a point in his favour.

The selection conference, evenly divided between union and ward delegates, took place in April 1968. Two of the nominees were unimpressive, it is recalled, a third was very young and inexperienced, and the fourth

---

[1]John Horam (Gateshead), Joe Dean (Leeds SW), Martin Flannery (Sheffield, Hillsborough) and Patrick Duffy (Sheffield, Attercliffe, formerly MP for Colne Valley), Joe Ashton (Bassetlaw), and Geoffrey Bing another former MP.

[2]Griffiths was sponsored by BISAKTA, the British Iron, Steel and Kindred Trades Association, now known as the ISTC or Iron and Steel Trades Confederation.

was local – Sheffield constituencies had a strong tradition of never select-ing a local man. Griffiths, who was quite unknown to all of those present, was an excellent speaker – 'silvery-tongued' one of those present remembered – and he impressed a majority of the committee with his rhetoric, his knowledge of the steel industry and his working-class back-ground – his father had been a miner. He was accordingly selected, but only narrowly. The youngest nominee was only about two votes behind. Whether an earlier problem over the AUEW nominee had anything to do with either the narrowness of the vote or the fact that it went to Griffiths, it is impossible to judge.

The new candidate for Brightside was 38 years old, an industrial chemist and an employee of the British Steel Corporation. He had stood as Labour candidate at Denbigh in 1966, coming third, and had also been a Labour member of Flintshire County Council in 1964. The Brightside by-election campaign was overshadowed for a time by the imminent local elections, due in early May. When the campaign got into full swing at the end of May, it was clear that the Labour Party was 'running scared' (Sheffield *Star*, 27 May 1968). One newspaper report said that both main parties were attacking the campaign as though Brightside were a marginal seat. With the disastrous local election results now known, and the un-popularity both of the Labour government at Westminster and of the Town Hall, it was clearly a difficult campaign to fight. This was made worse by the strength of the tenants' associations, who were threatening to put up a candidate of their own, but in the end were prevented by lack of funds. However, in addition to a Conservative and a Communist, Griffiths faced an independent candidate who had some support from the Shire-green Tenants' Association. This man, Colonel Lambert, was a Sheffield man, whose sympathies were basically Conservative, and who supported the tenants and also argued that someone with knowledge of the local steel industry was what Brightside needed. A latecomer was a second independ-ent, called Guest, a local chimneysweep, who expressed his dissatisfaction with all the existing parties.

All of these candidates wanted to take advantage of Labour's unpopular-ity. The Labour response was twofold. First, to roll up the big guns as supporting speakers in the shape of ministers and ex-ministers. Second, instead of facing the current problems, there was a harking back to the past. The campaign was deeply nostalgic in tone. Griffiths invoked the spirit of Keir Hardie, spoke of loyalty and faith. There was an effort to present Griffiths as a second Dick Winterbottom; the letter of support from the Prime Minister, Harold Wilson, to Griffiths praised Winter-bottom – 'A fine MP who gave to his constituents the devoted attention they required and deserved.' There was, however, no detectable sign of a loyalty vote in memory of Winterbottom, though Griffiths claimed there was 'a tremendous loyalty in the over 55s' (Sheffield *Star*, 11 June 1968).

In spite of much effort put in by all parties, the campaign remained lack-lustre. When the rare sparks flew it was usually between Griffiths and Wilkinson, the Communist candidate. Griffiths accused Wilkinson of being 'irresponsible' on steel, and in return Wilkinson called Griffiths 'the smuggest Labour candidate' he had never encountered, out of touch with the Sheffield steel industry, and failing to support the clerical workers' union in their fight for recognition at BSC (Sheffield *Morning Telegraph*, 11 June 1968). Griffiths gave a hostage to fortune which he later had cause to regret when early in the campaign he made a public promise to move into the constituency after the election. He also said, at the same press conference, that he had won the nomination because of his trade union background in the steel industry and that the selection conference had not been concerned about 'intellectual socialism' (Sheffield *Morning Tele-graph*, 11 June 1968).

The appeal to traditional values and loyalties and to the spirit of Keir Hardie evidently fell on many deaf ears. Massive abstentions by Labour voters were the most striking features of the result when it was announced.

In a low poll – only a 50 per cent turn out – none of the other candidates had succeeded in capitalising on Labour's unpopularity. The Com-munist's 1000 votes was about normal, and the Conservative vote rose by only 1500 compared with the General Election of 1966. The Independ-ents gained only 1500 votes between them. Yet Winterbottom's majority of more than 19,000 was slashed to little more than 5000. This meant that approximately 12,000 people who had voted for Winterbottom in March 1966 failed to vote for Griffiths in June 1968: the massive fall-off in Labour support seen by Hindess in Liverpool was shown here too.

For the next few years, Griffiths was an uncontroversial MP, who made little impact in Parliament. Nor does he seem to have made much impact in the constituency. The opportunity to make his maiden speech came within a month of his election to the Commons in a debate on the steel industry. Such speeches are by tradition non-controversial. Griffiths' speech was especially anodyne, ringing with the tones of the chapel, paying tribute to the 'warmth of character' of his constituents and quoting from the Bible. This 'apolitical' attitude was seen in many of his parlia-mentary contributions, which were usually limited to the subject of steel, with occasional speeches on pensions and only brief interventions on other matters. He was, however, one of a large group of MPs who in 1969 defied the party whips to vote against the White Paper *In Place of Strife* and also against the reintroduction of NHS charges.

Although the Labour government lost the 1970 general election, Griffiths' own result in Brightside showed an improvement on the poor 1968 by-election result, his majority rising to more than 15,000 and

Labour gaining 72 per cent of the vote. During the campaign Griffiths re-iterated his 1968 promise to move house and live in the constituency, which had still not been fulfilled.

But the loss of office marked a turning point in the party, as we have seen elsewhere. The old consensus in British politics had begun to die. The Heath Government's industrial relations legislation and the Housing Finance Act sharpened conflict. Within the party, too, the old traditions of loyalty and deference were becoming weaker. MPs were increasingly under attack from the rank and file. The election of Jones and Hugh Scanlon to head two of the most powerful unions – the dominant unions in Sheffield – marked a new leftward swing within the trade union movement.

The Common Market issue, too, was becoming an explosive one within the party, and indeed it was this issue which raised the question of the role of MPs *vis-à-vis* their local parties, which was to be so publicly debated at Lincoln from 1971 to 1973. The action of the sixty-nine MPs who voted in the Conservative lobby in favour of Common Market entry angered many on the left of the party, and provided some of the inspiration for the demands for reselection which would soon be heard. The Brightside constituency was, of course, not immune from these changes within the Labour Party as a whole. The growing strength of the AUEW and the increased radicalism of party activists made itself felt. A gulf began to appear between Griffiths and some of his local party members, especially from 1973 when the left made progress in Brightside. A left-wing chairman and secretary were elected, and new members recruited in the first big canvassing effort for many years. Some came from the tenants' movement, and some were shop stewards: there were others who had been in the party for some time. All were disillusioned not only with the leadership of Harold Wilson and the Labour government's record of 1964–70, but also with the way the Brightside party was run. It was inefficiently organised and more like 'an elderly women's knitting circle'[1] than a political party. There were financial muddles, over the sponsorship money from BISAKTA and over the bingo money.

Neither Griffiths nor his agent seemed able to cope with this influx of new members and the discontent of some older members. They knew there were problems but did not succeed in solving them. One prominent member of the group that later worked to get rid of Griffiths had allegedly told him that his union, the AUEW, did not approve of Griffiths, and might try to replace him. If there were any efforts to organise support for Griffiths to counter this, they were not successful. Gradually, a long list of discontents built up against the MP. Each on its own did not amount to

[1] J. Foster, 'The Brightside Affair', Sheffield *Morning Telegraph*, 27 August 1974.

much, but together they were enough to enable the left to move against him.

First, there was the house question. Griffiths had failed to keep his promise to live in the constituency, made at his selection, in the 1968 by-election campaign, and again in the 1970 general election campaign. He had looked at a large number of houses and rejected them all. This issue was of substantive importance to some, while others felt that the promise, so vehemently made, should be kept. Griffiths became very defensive on the subject, and refused to be challenged on it. Partly as a result of *not* living in Brightside and, therefore, having to make long journeys between London, Sheffield and North Wales, where his home was, he had failed to get closely involved in the constituency and had not built up a circle of friends in the local party. He did not often attend the GMC meetings, set for Friday evenings to enable the MP to come.

Secondly, he was said to have been dilatory over dealing with some constituents' cases. Griffiths held regular surgeries, and visited the constituency almost every weekend, but this was not enough to keep in close contact and keep his finger on the pulse of the CLP. One of his chief critics said that his contacts with local councillors were poor. He did not pass on cases as Winterbottom had; it was alleged that he would take up a case, usually concerned with housing, when things were quiet, and 'start slamming the local authority'. There were differences of opinion, however, on this matter. Some said that he was a very good constituency MP in this respect.

Thirdly, his parliamentary work was felt by some to be inadequate. His contributions were not sparkling ones, but his voting record was no worse than average, and he always spoke, as he said later, in steel debates. These speeches were good; often very technical in content, but nearly always following a pro-management line. This seems to have become more marked as time went on. His last speech in the House in February 1973 was in a debate on a ten-year strategy for BSC (Hansard, Commons, vol. 85, cols. 343-362). The Minister, Peter Walker, announced a £3000m modernisation plan. The opposition spokesman, Eric Varley, said that after 'two-and-a -half years of humiliation and harrassment' for BSC, Walker was being less than honest about the number of redundancies the plan would entail. Griffiths, on the other hand, welcomed the statement and favoured early retirement schemes to help cope with redundancies. He also favoured a sympathetic approach to the private sector. What emphasised Griffiths' distance from his own party was that no fewer than three Conservatives, including Walker, referred to his views in glowing terms. One said he spoke 'more sense than the whole of his front bench put together'. After this, Griffiths never spoke again in the House, although there remained eighteen months in which he continued as MP. This lack of parliamentary influence was not important to all the active members of the Brightside party; for some, it was enough to support the party.

Apart from these fairly general complaints, there were specific ones on policy issues which dated back to 1971. The first of these was the Common Market; a strong campaign against British entry had been mounted in Sheffield. Griffiths had declared himself to be 'on balance in favour', while the CLP was firmly opposed. Griffiths had refused to be influenced by this at a special meeting, but had taken 'soundings' in the constituency. These, too, indicated opposition and Griffiths voted against entry, but had irritated people a good deal. The Common Market issue reasserted itself in 1973. Griffiths is said to have threatened the GMC with parliamentary privilege. There had also been disagreements over a 'day of action' against the Heath Government's Industrial Relations Act and on a BSC rationalisation scheme in 1971. This included a proposal that Firth Brown, a private steel company, should take over BSC's River Don works, and other plans to 'hive off' profitable sectors of BSC to the private sector, with the possible loss of 3000 jobs. Griffiths had opposed these plans in the house, in a good speech,[1] but had failed to associate himself with an occupation of the works when milder methods had failed to change the plan. This action, described as 'one of the most remarkable trade union campaigns ever mounted in Sheffield' (Frazer Wright, Sheffield *Morning Telegraph*, 19 November 1975), was successful. The government, concerned as unemployment rose towards the one million mark, changed its mind, and the River Don Works went on to considerable, if short-lived, success. Other controversial local causes such as the action by the Clay Cross councillors following the Housing Finance Act, which were supported by the CLP, were not favoured by Griffiths. Apart from policy, there were several smaller grievances, such as failing to attend May Day rallies and dances. There was, therefore, an accumulation of discontents, some of them minor, which indicated a lack of sympathy between a basically apolitical MP and his by now thoroughly political, and left-wing, local party.

Griffiths' personality, as much as his political views or lack of them, contributed to this. Though he could turn on the charm, and could be an eloquent speaker, he was also seen by some as insecure and defensive, and did not pay enough attention to the small courtesies which are so important in constituency life. In addition to this, contacts with him became more difficult and sometimes even his agent could not contact him. Personal failings contributed to the general dissatisfaction. By the end of 1973 relations between Griffiths and the local party were severely strained; it was no longer the same party which had selected him and many

[1]Hansard, Commons, May 1971, vol. 818, cols. 117–123.

were not prepared to put up with what they saw as Griffiths' shortcomings as an MP.

In September 1973 the first indications appeared in the press that all was not well in Brightside. A special GMC meeting was called at which Griffiths was asked to explain why he had not kept his promise to move house. His children were at an important stage in their education, he said, and could not be moved. He told the press that he was suspicious of his critics' motives, adding 'It makes me wonder – this is the first time in five years that matters raised at these meetings have been got into the press.' Although a no-confidence vote was not taken, there does appear to have been a vote of some kind, which was a tie, and Griffiths was reminded that his 1968 promise to live in the constituency had contributed to his selection.

Griffiths made some attempt to rally support to himself after this, but found he was under strong attack from the left. He did not work well under pressure and, therefore, found it difficult to cope with the crisis, but also lacked a power base in the constituency. In addition to this, he did not believe that any attempt to dismiss him could succeed. As time went on, his support weakened, partly because the left grew stronger, but also because Griffiths' own supporters left him. A group of perhaps twelve people were now determined to get rid of Griffiths. At the annual general meeting of the Brightside party in February 1974, the agent resigned his post of secretary and made way for an ambitious young left-winger, Clive Betts, having first failed in an attempt to postpone the meeting because a general election had been called.

By the time of the February 1974 general election the rupture between Griffiths and most of the general management committee was virtually complete. It seems that an attempt by one of the ward parties to move a resolution of no-confidence in him was started, but then put a stop to, because it was felt that their case against the MP was too weak. In any event, it was with reluctance that the local party worked for him in that campaign. This was yet a further cause for ill-feeling. It had long been a tradition that in Brightside, so safely Labour, campaigning was left to the last few days before the election. Up till then, party workers went further afield, helping their colleagues in more marginal constituencies, in Sheffield and elsewhere. Griffiths objected to this, and refused to take part in it. He also refused to hold public meetings, preferring 'coffee mornings' in private houses. It does seem that on this occasion the tradition became, for some at least, an excuse to do very little for an MP they no longer supported, preferring to work in the very marginal High Peak constituency.

There were other irritants: he made a speech at Firth Brown on the need for an incomes policy, and was also alleged to have attacked the miners, whose confrontation with the Heath Government was the cause of the election. He was being 'frozen out', and for Griffiths himself the strongest evidence of this came on the day after the election – at which he had improved his majority by 5000 votes – at a 'victory dinner'. Griffiths found that Peter Jackson, former High Peak MP, was also present and was deeply upset when Jackson made a speech which was enthusiastically received, while Griffiths was offered no wine (a sign of the times!) and was not congratulated on his record result.[1] Thus Griffiths gave the appearance of being unduly sensitive, while the local party members appeared to him at least, not to pay him the attention he felt was his due.

After the election, a Labour Government was formed, but it had no House of Commons majority. It was therefore walking a continual tightrope in the House of Commons, and it was clearly only a matter of months before another general election. Similarly, in Brightside, the local party was waiting for an opportunity to make another move against Griffiths. The chance for this came in the spring. In April, Griffiths spent a weekend at the home of his House of Commons 'pair', Ernle Money, the Conservative MP for Ipswich. Photographs of the two at a Junior Chamber of Commerce ball appeared in the local press (and subsequently in the national press). They also attended a football match and a church service together. While Griffiths was at the ball, Michael Foot was addressing five hundred members of the Ipswich Labour Party. Ipswich was the third most marginal Conservative seat in the country – indeed Money was, like Griffiths, to lose his seat at the next election. The local Labour Party, understandably, was annoyed at Griffiths' behaviour. A protest was sent to Transport House, and also to the Brightside party. Griffiths' ill-advised conduct was just what they had been waiting for: for the Brightside GMC, the Ipswich visit became 'a peg on which to hang their dissatisfaction' (Sheffield *Morning Telegraph*, 27 August 1974).

Griffiths was hauled over the coals by the GMC at a meeting on 14 June. A no confidence resolution was passed, but only on the casting vote of the chairman. The matter was referred to the executive committee, and it was agreed to maintain silence on the matter. It was also agreed to hold two subsequent meetings, in July and September, in accordance with the Labour Party rules for such disputes, as amended in 1970. Since Griffiths did not feel bound to keep silent, the press got hold of the story. He said that he expected 'a bad result' at the scheduled meetings, which would be 'packed' by his opponents (Sheffield *Star*, 24 June 1974; *Daily Mail*, 28 June 1974). His difficulties had nothing to do with the Ipswich visit, he said, but were a result of left-wing domination of the party, largely due to the AUEW and TGWU.

---

[1] In fact, boundary changes had added to the safe Labour votes in Brightside.

At the next executive meeting (5 July) the matter was again discussed. Griffiths, though invited, did not attend. The regional organiser, who was present, prevented a no confidence vote from being taken. Secrecy was pledged once again, and once again, after the meeting, Griffiths attacked his opponents, as 'a handful of extremists' (Sheffield *Star*, 6 July 1974). The agent supported him, attributing Griffiths' problems to the fact that he was sponsored by BISAKTA and the AUEW wanted control. These remarks seem only to have stiffened the hostility towards him, and when the GMC met on 19 July, the vote went against him 40–12.

The crucial meeting had been meticulously prepared for. The party secretary sent a letter to each delegate, informing them of the date and time, reminding them to bring their current party membership cards, and pointing out the agreement not to comment to the press or other media. These letters were each delivered by hand, by two people. This is a measure of the care that was taken to ensure that all the party rules were complied with.[1] Fifty-two delegates turned up, as well as the regional organiser who was obliged by the party rules to oversee the whole business very carefully, and Griffiths himself. Feelings were running high, mainly because of pressure from news reporters, who were excluded from the hall, and with whom an angry scene took place.

Before the meeting was the recommendation from the executive committee that Griffiths should retire at the next general election. It had to be decided whether a further GMC on 6 September should consider that question. Procedural matters were dealt with first. Griffiths attempted to have the debate limited to the Ipswich affair, which had been the subject of the previous GMC meeting, but he was overruled. When the debate proper started, Griffiths spoke first, and at length. He dwelt mainly on his dismay and anger at the whole matter, and on the Ipswich visit and the 1 March victory dinner. He referred continually to the meeting as a 'trial', and attacked some members for having, he said, supported Lambert in the 1968 by-election.[2] It was he who was loyal to the Labour Party, not they, he said, and he could see many new faces present. It was not a performance which much impressed his audience.

In the general debate which followed, it was clear that most of the committee was in favour of replacing Griffiths. Those who supported him defended his loyalty to the party line in Parliament, and one ward chairman said that his ward had passed a resolution expressing their support for

---

[1]There had been some contact with the Lincoln Labour Party on procedure; several of the active members had campaigned for the Labour Party in Lincoln in the March 1973 by-election.

[2]One of the criticisms of Griffiths was that he had attacked the tenants' associations.

the MP. For the most part, however, this was not the case; speaker after speaker attacked Griffiths. Some brought up the various points of dissension mentioned earlier, others were evidently very hostile because of Griffiths' recent public attacks on the party. 'The last few days had finally clinched the argument', said one. More striking was the evidence that many viewed the party in a different way from their MP; several declared themselves 'left-wing' and proud of it. One speaker said she was in the party to see change, 'and change would be achieved by being radical, and not by being a silent moderate'. Griffiths, she added, did not represent the feelings and aspirations of the GMC. Again, another said:

> 'Many people in the constituency who once supported Eddie Griffiths are now totally disillusioned with what he was doing, both in and out of Parliament.'

In addition, Griffiths' lack of skill in dealing with his constituents came out. One member, who deplored the rift in the party, advised him to 'take a course in human relationships. Griffiths' speech in reply to the discussion repeated what he had said earlier. He clearly felt he was being unjustly attacked. All accusations against him were half truth and innuendo, he said.

The vote went against him 40–12. It was then agreed that the chairman and regional organiser should make a press statement 'as and when necessary'. Once again, Griffiths reserved his right to speak to the press, as he was not a delegate to the GMC. He did so, describing what had happened as a 'well planned coup', instigated by a small group of young left-wing extremists. 'My enemies have been massing their forces against me', he was quoted as saying, and predicted that their next choice for MP would be 'a real left-winger'. While his language was somewhat dramatic, the prediction was correct.

In the interval between the first and second meetings, necessary under Labour Party rules, Griffiths finally moved to a house just outside the constituency boundary, which might have been expected to count in his favour, but at the same time, a petition organised by the agent had difficulty in raising 1000 signatures in his support. On the national scene, the government suffered a serious defeat in the Commons, bringing a new election significantly nearer. The second meeting itself appears to have been little more than a formality. Griffiths himself was not present and the vote was very similar to the previous one – 40 to 10 in favour of his retirement. The last stage in the dismissal procedure was the appeal to the NEC. This was heard on 11 September, considerably sooner than would normally have been the case, because of the imminence of a general election.

Griffiths had said ever since the dispute became public that he would take the fight 'to the top', to the NEC. But it was clear that the only role which that body could play in an affair of this kind was that of checking that all the party rules had been complied with, in other words to ensure that the dismissal was constitutional. The utmost care had been taken by the Brightside party, especially the secretary, to ensure that every action they took would be entirely within the rules. So, the rejection of the appeal was again a mere formality. It was heard by the organisation sub-committee of the NEC, of whose seventeen members only three were present, Ian Mikardo, Bryan Stanley and Tom Bradley. They were unanimous, stating that 'as the procedures carried out were strictly in accordance with the party constitution Mr Griffiths' appeal is not upheld'. The committee added that it would be highly desirable for his name to be included in the shortlist for the selection of a new candidate.

Griffiths was bitterly disappointed at the decision, and at the committee's refusal to look at the facts rather than merely at the procedural details. 'I came to London looking for justice, and found instead that the only thing that mattered was procedure,' he said (*The Times*, 12 September 1974).

The Brightside party now had to choose a new candidate. From a large number of applications, a shortlist of five was drawn up on 15 September. Since Griffiths had declined to allow his name to go forward, and the dismissal procedure was now complete, the party now broke its long silence and issued, at the same time, a 600-word statement explaining the reasons for its action. Most of these have already been discussed, but there are two general accusations which were important. The first was that he adopted a lifestyle unsuitable to a Labour MP. There is no doubt that some of the party objected strongly to things such as the visit to Ipswich. Griffiths, defending himself, acknowledged that he might have annoyed some by the invitations which he accepted, 'but it is an MP's duty to represent all shades of opinion in the constituency and not just the left-wingers' (Sheffield *Star*, 16 September 1974). He went on: 'The Brightside party's thinking seems to be that unless you have a cloth cap, a muffler and a boiler suit, you are not fit to be a Labour MP'. (Sheffield *Morning Telegraph*, 17 September 1974.) There is evidence, however, that there was more to the accusation than this, and that the dislike of Griffiths was based on other than political matters.

Secondly, he was accused of 'failing to give a political lead'. Griffiths denied this, saying, though that he had refused 'to follow the lunatic fringe in associating myself with every revolutionary, Trotskyite and International Marxist cause that came along. I am a loyal member of the Labour party,' (Sheffield *Morning Telegraph*, 17 September 1974). This remark may be taken as an indication of how far removed he was politically from the leading members of the Brightside party and of the fact that he, himself, was not above using an occasional innuendo.

Meanwhile, the task of choosing a new candidate got under way. The shortlist of five consisted of three councillors, plus two others. These were: Peter Jackson, former MP for High Peak, well-known to some in the Brightside party and Joan Maynard, sponsored by the Agricultural Workers' Union, a member of the NEC and well-known left-winger. The party was taking no chances with this selection; 'we didn't want any surprises' said one. Any of the five would have been acceptable to the leaders, although the tradition of not choosing a local man made the three councillors look as though they were only there to make up the numbers. At least one of them had no illusions about this. It was, therefore, really a contest between Peter Jackson and Joan Maynard.

The day before the selection conference took place, the Brightside party distributed a hastily printed leaflet in the constituency. In some parts barely legible, it was entitled 'Why a new MP for Brightside?' and called for an MP who would be active, inside and outside Parliament, live in the constituency, oppose the Common Market and compulsory wages policies, cooperate with the unions and local councillors and hold regular public meetings, in other words, someone who would be everything that Eddie Griffiths was not.

Joan Maynard had been tipped by the press as the favourite to gain the nomination shortly before the selection took place. Although Peter Jackson was on good terms with the leading members of the Brightside GMC, when it came to the selection two things spoiled his chances. One was the revelation of an association with the Liberal Party. While an MP he had written an article proposing an alliance between radicals in both parties. Secondly, although he had chalked up more anti-Government votes than practically any other MP between 1966 and 1970, he was less concerned with the 'bread and butter issues' of politics dearest to the hearts of the Brightside members. In addition to this, the ground had been excellently prepared for Miss Maynard. She was only approached shortly before the shortlisting took place, but a number of influential people, chiefly AUEW members, had worked assiduously on her behalf. Only one ballot was necessary to secure her selection, although several of those most active in the removal of Griffiths did not vote for her and most of the GMC had never seen her before. The pro-Griffiths faction on the GMC probably voted for Jackson, whom they saw as the inevitable choice. Miss Maynard's selection prompted this group to support an independent candidacy by Griffiths, and claimed forty members split away to join them.

The campaign was an unpleasant one. Griffiths persistently attacked Miss Maynard as an extremist, making play of the fact that a Communist was not standing. The Labour Party closed ranks around her quite effectively; support for her came from several MPs, the AUEW and, more surprisingly, the ISTC, Griffiths' sponsoring union. Those who came to speak for her included two local MPs, Fred Mulley and Patrick Duffy. Griffiths attacked this in a characteristic way; he accused the CLP of importing speakers they despised. Two such moderates he said, 'would not normally be allowed within five miles of Brightside'.

Griffiths additionally irritated the local party by refusing to use the term independent. This undoubtedly confused voters. The theme of his election address was 'stand by Eddie Griffiths', and in it he reiterated his charge that only a few families controlled the local party. He also, incidentally, called for the reintroduction of birching. The confusion was illustrated by rival advertisements in the local press, Miss Maynard's describing her as 'the only official Labour party candidate in Brightside', and Griffiths replying with one which called on the electorate to 'stand up and be counted with Eddie Griffiths your Labour candidate'.

There was a good deal of ill-feeling at the count, various sorts of 'dirty tricks' being alleged, but the result itself was one which the Brightside party viewed with relief rather than dismay, in spite of the impact of Griffiths. The nature of his attacks on Miss Maynard and the coverage given to them by the press had made them fear that their candidate might actually lose.

Miss Maynard received more than 18,000 votes, Griffiths more than 10,000. The combined Liberal and Conservative vote had fallen by nearly 4000. Heath's confrontation with the miners no doubt accounted for some of the lost Conservative votes, but Griffiths probably gained quite a few from both parties. In spite of Griffiths' 10,000 votes, Miss Maynard had more votes than Griffiths got in 1968 and a bigger majority, too.

A concluding look at Griffiths and the problems he faced must have two facets. First, he was not Dick Winterbottom, and never managed to replace him for the party faithful. Nor could he satisfy the newer, more left-wing members of the party. It might be said that his personality was not suited to withstand the constant criticism which is a necessary part of the process of accountability between MP and local party, or to cope with the crises which arise within that relationship. The opinion was also expressed by several of those involved that he was not naturally gregarious and did not easily make friends either in the constituency or in Parliament. Apart from the house question and the Ipswich visit, his sins were mainly those of omission rather than commission. Though his parliamentary record was unimpressive, he worked hard if not always effectively on constituents' problems, but the other side of his extra-parliamentary work – championing local causes etc. was not good, unlike Winterbottom's – and he rarely attended party meetings. He never sought a battle with his constituency party, unlike Taverne, and could not be accused of going against their wishes in any parliamentary division. Other comparisons with Taverne might be made. Taverne detected tensions from the start of his connection with the Lincoln Labour Party. While this does not seem to have been the case with Griffiths, the vote that selected him was a very narrow one, and one speaker at the July 1974 GMC meeting brought this up, suggesting that the party had been divided all along. Lincoln, unlike Brightside, was vulnerable to a challenge from the Conservatives (indeed it was a seat they gained at the 1979 general election), and Taverne faced a political and social milieu very different from that of Brightside, one which included many potential social democrats, who offered him considerable support in his fight. Taverne also had abundant talent and many friends, some of them prominent in the parliamentary party, or in the 'establishment'. Not a single MP spoke out in support of Griffiths.

As we have seen, the local party which dismissed Griffiths in 1974 was not the same party which had selected him in 1968. There had been quite a turnover of membership as old people died or retired and new, mainly younger, members joined, accompanied by a change of view among some long-established members.[1] So, as with other constituencies all over the country, the general political stance of the party moved leftward. Quite a few of the new, or newly active, were also AUEW members, but the influence of the union should not be exaggerated. The union does not dominate as much as it might – for example, its nominee has never been selected as a parliamentary candidate. Labour politics in Brightside is very much a family affair; one member said that 60 per cent of activists are husbands and wives. Certainly, the GMC has quite a few couples among its membership – this was also true in 1974, and not all were opposed to Griffiths. This is, contrary to what Griffiths implied in his speeches and press comments, not unusual in Sheffield or in other northern Labour strongholds.[2] So, Griffiths' accusations were a little wild; but he spoke the truth when he said that there was a small group who had worked to oust him. However, the left-wingers – or rather the group who were mainly responsible for the dismissal, for Brightside contained no social democrats – were not strong enough on their own to win the vote in the GMC. Other factors were involved. David Butler strongly contends that personal rather than ideological considerations – in his words, 'drink, divorce or neglect of constituency business' (1978) – are responsible for most constituency–party MP conflicts. The Brightside affair would appear to be a mixture of the two. Those who defended Griffiths did so from motives of

---

[1]In 1981 only two *active* members remained who had been on the 1968 selection committee – a married couple, far from young, and fairly left-wing in their views.
[2]In Clay Cross, one family, the Skinners, dominates politics. This is also true in Stockton-on-Tees (*Sunday Times*, February 1981).

loyalty because he was the MP, mixed in some cases with resentment or a dislike of the methods that were used. Griffiths might have survived a vote by the whole membership.

The bitterness aroused by the affair was deep. The Brightside GMC felt hounded by the press, and the most prominent had been subject to anonymous phone calls and public abuse. The result of this was a close solidarity – 'like being in the war' one said. Another spoke about it in the re-selection debate at the annual conference a few months later:

> Dirt is thrown around, people are accused, you cannot walk down the streets without people accusing you of being Marxists, International Socialists. Everything is thrown at you. (Labour Party Annual Conference Report 1974, p. 173.)

It must be said that although the affair reflected changes that were taking place in constituency parties all across the country, and the actions of the small group of activists involved in the ousting of Griffiths were influenced by what they had seen in Lincoln, and perhaps by the newly-founded Campaign for Labour Party Democracy, and although in addition, they had to a certain extent revived a torpid party, there was no question of any infiltration by outsiders, or of any activity by groups such as the Militant Tendency. Griffiths' remarks in the election campaign implied that this might have been the case. Indeed he made powerful use of a piece of right-wing mythology observed also in the Liverpool study quoted above; the feeling that 'anyone who tries to stir up political activity must be a troublemaker' (Hindess, 1971, p. 108), that all dissidents must be Trotskyites.

Although the case was part of a trend which was to become more marked as time went on – exemplified best by the fact that the activists and the MP seemed to be speaking different political languages – it must not be forgotten that Griffiths' personal failings were an important contributory factor. Support for him both in and out of the CLP was minimal. This was not the case in other disputes, and may be one reason why the activists were successful in getting rid of their MP in an unusually short time. Another reason for their success was the extreme care which was taken on the procedural aspects of the dismissal. As Hindess observed, and as was to become noticeable later in a wider context, 'the party constitution acts as a very useful and effective weapon in the hands of those who are most familiar with them' (1971, p. 115).

The group of activists formed a fairly homogeneous group, more so one suspects than most CLP leaderships, and they succeeded to a remarkable degree in keeping to their self-imposed silence, though they were also very frank in answering questions on the affair when several years had elapsed. What must distinguish them is their unequivocal determination to get rid of Griffiths. Unlike most such groups, they included a number of ambitious, occasionally ruthless people, some of whom have since made rapid progress in city politics, and have come to occupy positions of power. Some are now themselves actual or potential parliamentary candidates.

The Griffiths case was one of the first to pinpoint the issue which has subsequently grown to be of central concern in the Labour party: the power of the activists. Although it may be argued that they were justified and certainly they acted with constitutional propriety, it was nonetheless a tiny group, acting more or less alone, and without reference to the broader constituency, which unseated Eddie Griffiths and put Joan Maynard in his place.

8 The campaign for mandatory reselection

As a result of the developments of the early 1970s, and the efforts of the CLPD, the idea of exerting greater control over MPs had become an issue of growing importance within the Labour Party, but it was not debated at the annual conference until 1974. That year, because of the general election which had been held in October, the conference took place at the end of November and was shorter than usual, most of its time being taken up with a debate on party organisation and structure.[1] One aspect of this was the selection of parliamentary candidates; the NEC had produced a report on the subject, which concluded that the existing system of selection by a delegate conference should remain basically as it was, since this was thought to be the only method by which the affiliated organisations could 'take their rightful place' in the selection process. But 'topping up' of delegate lists would be stopped and improvements would be made in the information available on candidates both by means of a detailed questionnaire added to the nomination form and possibly by interviewing in advance of the selection procedure proper.

At the 1974 conference there were several interesting amendments to the NEC's endorsement of the *status quo* which indicated the lines of future debate within the party. One, from Chingford CLP, would have allowed ward members to attend a selection conference if they had been members for one year and had attended 75 per cent of ward meetings. Another, from Hammersmith North, Tomney's constituency, called for reselection to be possible at any time. The heart of the matter, as promoted by the CLPD, was contained in an amendment moved by Ken Coates, on behalf of Rushcliffe CLP; several other constituency parties, including Brightside, had withdrawn amendments in Rushcliffe's favour. It

[1]Area consultations involving nearly 3000 activists had taken place in 1972–3; reselection had been a live issue in these consultations (see Labour Party Annual Conference Report 1974, p. 36).

proposed that the selection procedure should take place before every general election, with the sitting MP automatically gaining a place on the short list. Coates distinguished two grounds on which CLPs might wish to remove a sitting member: political incompatibility, and 'other' reasons, and though he acknowledged that the second sort of reason was more common, he made it clear that for the left-wing activists this change would be a 'political commitment' by the party to increased accountability in political life as in other spheres. The general tone of the debate was unmistakable; MPs were seen as being 'divorced from the reality of the situation'. 'Many of our parliamentary candidates have risen above the movement', said one delegate. Resentment towards MPs showed through clearly, and the Common Market issue was mentioned more than once; the bitterness over the pro-Marketeers had not gone. A notable contribution to the debate was made by Peter Price, the delegate from Sheffield Brightside, who spoke of the unpleasant experiences of his local party at the time of the Griffiths affair. He said that the procedure necessary to get rid of a sitting MP went on for too long, adding that there was nothing worse than a local party putting up a man in whom they had no confidence. 'It breeds apathy, not only among the party workers, but among the electorate.' He finished by saying, 'If the parliamentarians are not going to take note of conference, then let us make them take note of the constituencies.'

The NEC opposed all the amendments which had been put forward, and Ian Mikardo, a co-author of the Tribune pamphlet published two years previously, was given the task of replying on behalf of the platform. In the words of *Socialist Commentary*, Mikardo 'sympathised with the most left-wing demands and ordered conference to reject them'. In what even *Tribune* described as a 'deeply reasoned argument', he stood by the *status quo* on the question of who should select candidates and while defending the right of a constituency party to sack its MP, said in effect that the present system was good enough. Citing the Lincoln and Brightside cases, he argued that selection was not in practice 'a ticket for life', and made it clear that the NEC's function in such cases should be to determine whether the procedure had been properly carried out. But divorce should not be easy, he said, it was a last resort. He also condemned the Chingford amendment; this would 'extend participation to those who do not do their share of the party's chores'.

Mikardo's arguments appeared to convince a majority of the conference. Although the proposition in favour of reselection received two million votes, more than three million were cast against it, and the amendments were defeated. But the CLPD continued its model resolution campaign; ten resolutions favouring mandatory reselection were put down in 1975 and thirty-six in 1976. These the Conference Arrangements Committee ruled out of order under the three-year rule. In both years, emergency resolutions were also refused. A resolution on 'party democracy' remitted to the NEC at the 1975 Conference got the same treatment. This resolution noted with alarm the government's failure to carry out conference decisions, and drew attention to the need to make the government accountable and to 'shift political decision-making in both national and local affairs to the activists and party members at grassroots level'. It wanted MPs to be accountable to local parties and subject to recall, as well as effective measures to ensure that the PLP carried out the decisions of the conference. The NEC reply in 1976 was that the main points had been covered by the 1974 amendments, and on this ground they refused to accept it. The inhibitions of some NEC critics of the Government, as well as the procedural rules, were probably behind this refusal. By 1977, however, the statutory three years had elapsed since the question had last been debated and it was widely accepted that a debate would be permitted at that year's conference.

In the interval there had been several highly-publicised challenges to sitting MPs, which lent weight to the arguments of those who favoured mandatory reselection and said that the dismissal procedure was too lengthy. One such dispute was that between Neville Sandelson and his constituency party at Hillingdon. He had first been elected MP in 1971 after the death of the previous MP, Arthur Skeffington. It was not his first attempt to gain a seat, and it was said that he won the nomination because the left wing in the constituency, where divisions between left and right went back many years, could not agree on a candidate. It is easy to see that Sandelson himself was not likely to appeal to the left as a candidate or MP. A founder-member of the Manifesto group, a Cambridge-educated barrister with a 'friendly but patrician manner', he encountered hostility from the beginning from the left-wingers in the party, especially the Hillingdon Trades Council. His relations with the constituents as a whole, however, were said to be excellent.

The first substantive source of friction was Sandelson's pro-EEC stance. He had made this clear before his selection, in his maiden speech in the House, and when he voted in the Conservative lobby in October 1971. Moves were made to oust him at this early stage, but none were successful. His support for the unpopular economic policies of the Government later won him more enemies and the strength of the left in the CLP grew, especially when Sandelson attacked the Shrewsbury pickets and led the pro-Prentice campaign in the Commons.

The moves against him first reached a peak at the end of 1976, when the press was full of reports about infiltration of local Labour parties by the Militant Tendency. The most surprising aspect of the case is that Sandelson gained the support of Callaghan, Foot and Hayward, all anxious not to face an embarrassing by-election with Sandelson standing as an Independent. In January 1977, he narrowly survived when his local party voted on a retirement motion. Again in 1979, a vote was taken but this time Sandelson lost. The NEC stepped in and endorsed him as the candidate for the May 1979 general election, a move they had cause to regret when he became one of the first Labour MPs to join the new Social Democratic Party. Long before, Sandelson's relations with his local party had become extremely acrimonious. He made many public attacks on the left-wing clique, which he said had taken over the party, and referred to his general management committee as 'half-wits' (*Financial Times*, 27 January 1981). In spite of some Militant activity there was little evidence of outsiders at work in the constituency, though the more conservative members were totally inactive.

If Sandelson's dispute was almost entirely political, this was not the case with Mrs Maureen Colquhoun. She fits more exactly the Butler formula of 'divorce, drink and personal considerations', but there were also political differences between the MP and her Northampton North constituency party. Her frequent public outbursts, several embarrassing incidents and her declared homosexuality led to a considerable amount of adverse publicity in 1976, which would have been enough to cause concern in the local party, but she also encountered hostility from her Tribune group colleagues in 1977 when she appeared to support Enoch Powell's views on race, and said 'It is impossible to talk about race in the Labour party for fear of being labelled a racialist.' (*The Times*, 4 May 1977.) In addition, it seems likely that she offended middle-of-the-road Labour voters in her constituency by her support for the 'Troops Out' movement and her association with those who protested against the treatment of IRA prisoners.

Several separate attempts to remove her were unsuccessful. The first started after the 'Powell affair' in January 1977, but her appeal to the NEC was successful. Dismissal proceedings were immediately restarted, but the 1979 general election intervened, and she was readopted for the highly marginal seat, which fell to the Conservatives.

The greatest amount of publicity had, however, been devoted to the case of Reg Prentice. This was a 'gift' to the CLPD. Following his dismissal by his Newham North East constituency party, his attempt to appeal to the 1976 conference had been ruled out of order. A month later, he left the Transport and General Workers' Union, which sponsored him, and then the Cabinet. Finally in October 1977 he joined the Conservative Party. Those prominent members of the Government who had supported him were deeply embarrassed, while the supporters of mandatory reselection were jubilant.

CLPD had been active in the unions as well as in constituency parties in

1975 and 1976, and had also been lobbying the NEC. But at the same time as these events favoured the proponents of reform, the right in the party was becoming increasingly concerned about infiltration of the party by extreme left-wingers. The Newham North East party was said to have been the target of 'entryism', but the NEC had not permitted the publication of the report on the subject by Lord Underhill. Wilson and Callaghan both attacked infiltrators, and succeeded in identifying the campaign for reselection with extremism: at the 1975 conference Wilson had asked

> who are these self-appointed Samurai who seek to assert a power of political life or death which the leadership of this party and Whips' Office and the Organisation Subcommittee of the Labour party have not in modern times sought to assert? (Wilson, 1979, p. 299.)

The issue had thus become a highly sensitive one, and although the NEC was by now thought to favour mandatory reselection, it seems to have gone to some lengths to prevent the issue being properly debated at the 1977 conference. Under the procedure agreed for constitutional proposals in 1968, it would have been remitted to the NEC for consideration and report back, and would therefore not be fully aired until 1978. A good deal of ill-feeling was aroused on the opening Monday morning session of the conference, when the Conference Arrangements Committee ruled out of order a series of emergency resolutions on the grounds that there were already resolutions on that subject on the agenda. This ruling was immediately challenged by a delegate from Kensington CLP and a leading figure in the CLPD. He said that seventy-five resolutions on reselection were being 'swept under the carpet without debate'. An attempt was made to refer back the report of the Conference Arrangements Committee; although this failed, a card vote was necessary.[1]

The desire to prevent a debate did not originate only in procedure; the composite resolution which had found its way onto the agenda demanded not only automatic reselection after a maximum of forty-two months after a general election, but had added to it a further demand that in addition the GMC could hold a reselection conference at any time. This seems to have been the result of overenthusiastic pressure by some members of the Militant Tendency, rather than the CLPD. It was definitely not acceptable to the NEC, and would probably not have had much chance of being carried. However, it may have been as a result of the strong feelings

---

[1] *Tribune* calculated, how accurately it is impossible to tell, that with only NUPE and ASTMS among the larger unions supporting a wider discussion of the subject, that 80 per cent of the CLPs must have supported it. Most of the emergency resolutions came from constituencies that were Conservative strongholds.

expressed on the Monday morning that, when the composite resolution came up for discussion in the private session later in the week, that Ian Mikardo, for the NEC gave a firm commitment that at the 1978 conference the Executive would produce proposals to provide automatic reselection 'in the way and in the sense' that the sponsors of the resolutions wanted. He added 'I do not think that there is the least chance of the Executive reneging on that undertaking.'

That, however, is exactly what many thought had happened when the 1978 conference met. The NEC, clearly divided on the reselection issue, had in the intervening year set up a working party to examine the issue. The resulting report proposed not the automatic and mandatory reselection for which the CLPD had been campaigning, but a compromise which had apparently been inspired by Joe Ashton, though it came to be named after Mikardo, who paid the price of losing his seat on the NEC. The compromise 'Mikardo' formula consisted of a two-stage procedure, whereby a CLP would hold a meeting to decide whether it was satisfied with its MP, and if not go on to reselect. Many who favoured reselection thought this inadequate; these included some members of the NEC working party, Eric Heffer among them, who submitted a minority report along the lines favoured by the many CLPs who had submitted resolutions on the subject in 1977.

The chief criticism made in the minority report (Labour Party Annual Conference Report 1978, pp. 448–9) was that the section of the rules under which the sackings of the 1970s had been possible would disappear. This section provided for a local party to initiate dismissal proceedings at any time if this were thought necessary; the NEC proposals, on the other hand, would make permission from itself a necessary condition for such proceedings to be started if it were separate from the formal reselection process, which would take place not less than eighteen and not more than thirty-six months after the election. In other words, the minority report wanted reselection to be possible at any time, while the NEC proposals sought to limit this to exceptional circumstances.

The NEC proposals were also strongly criticised by other speakers from the floor. They would, claimed one, 'reproduce exactly the problems, the bitterness and the divisions experienced at Newham and elsewhere' (Labour Party Annual Conference Report 1978, p. 273). Reselection, in order to be a safe and democratic process, had to be the norm, argued this school of thought. Otherwise, 'the vultures of the media' would descend and make a meal of those cases in which reselection was decided on, and there would be 'mini-Newhams' up and down the country (Labour Party Annual Conference 1978, pp. 272 and 276).

'just think', said one delegate, 'how the NEC proposal gives an open invitation to the anti-Labour mass media to leap upon any constituency which opts to use the option, with stories of Red plots, subversives and so on'. (Labour Party Annual Conference Report 1978, p. 272.)

Joe Ashton was one of only two MPs to speak in the short debate. He strongly opposed automatic reselection, saying that MPs had as much right as any one else to say a few words in their defence, but also fearing widespread sackings.

'Nights of the long knives and the biggest purges that you have seen', he predicted, would split the party and would strongly discourage anyone from seeking candidacy in a marginal seat. He described the dilemma faced by MPs, which would only be exacerbated by the introduction of mandatory reselection:

> You are asking us to try all the time to serve five masters – to do what Conference tells us to do, to do what the constituency tells us to do, to do what our trade union tells us to do, to do what the government and the whips tell us. Then there is the electorate telling us what to do. (Labour Party Annual Conference Report 1978, p. 278.)

He thought the proposal, far from encouraging working-class candidates as its supporters maintained, would drive them out and favour the middle-class professional types: 'all you are doing is creating a better system for the public relations men, the journalists, the lawyers, all the whiz kids, the ones who can use the media'.

The reply from the platform by Bryan Stanley of the post office engineers' union, who had been chairman of the working party, indicated how much the NEC had been under pressure from the left. Members of Parliament, he said, are 'accountable to their constituencies, but that relationship is a very delicate relationship, and I must say that I do not like the atmosphere that grew into the debate this afternoon'. He felt that the accusations from the supporters of the CLPD that the NEC had not kept its promise were wrong, and defended the NEC's proposals as more democratic, adding a cutting remark, 'the CLPD had better change its name if it is going to persist with that point of view'. Feelings were therefore running very high on the issue; one observer described the mood as one of 'anti-authoritarian assertiveness by a rank-and-file demanding the accountability of its representatives, be it the platform or the PLP' (Patrick Wintour, *New Statesman*, 6 October 1978).

It seems that the Mikardo compromise was enough for many on the left; and it may be that some unions felt that they had defied the platform enough in rejecting the 5 per cent pay policy and the government's economic strategy. The vote did little to resolve the matter; indeed it revealed the shortcomings of the procedures of the Conference. There were approximately three million votes for the NEC proposals, with roughly two million against, but there was also extreme confusion surrounding the AUEW Engineering Section vote. The delegates of this group had apparently abstained in the vote on mandatory reselection although mandated to vote for it, and then voted for the NEC proposals although they were not mandated and should have abstained. Strong pressure was said to have been exerted on the rest of the delegation by Duffy and Scanlon, and a request was made the following day for the vote to be retaken, but amid uproar this was refused.

The resulting confusion meant that the issue remained unresolved. Mandatory reselection was finally to be voted part of the party's constitution at the 1979 conference. There were several factors at work which finally gave the CLPD what it had worked for for so long. Embarrassment over the 1978 vote played a part in this; Scanlon's 'mistake' caused resentment and appeared to have flouted the wishes of the conference, at which a majority of union mandates had favoured the more radical proposal. But there were also changes in the party which meant that the matter would be left to rest. Changes in NEC membership, especially in the CLP section of the committee, pushed it further to the left. By 1979, there were no right-wingers in this section and no shadow cabinet members were elected to the committee. The old Bevanites, Ian Mikardo and Barbara Castle, were no longer on the committee, and their places were taken by Dennis Skinner and Jo Richardson, both adherents of CLPD, and as a result the constituency section of the committee became more assertive than it had been in the past. Another NEC member, Joan Lestor, had been converted to the idea of mandatory reselection by assiduous lobbying by the CLPD who had kept up their campaign. Union affiliation changes also assisted the cause of the left – this probably added about half a million votes to their strength at the 1979 Conference.

In addition, after the 1979 election, Tony Benn became associated for the first time with the proposals for constitutional reform, from which he had hitherto held aloof. His support, even at this late date, must have given the campaign a major boost; indeed within a few months the press associated him almost exclusively with it.

The events of 1979 – the winter of discontent which followed the government's determination to stick to its five per cent pay policy, and the defeat in the general election in May – all contributed very importantly to the mood of the party activists and trade unionists, who now more strongly favoured control of the parliamentary party.

In the aftermath of the election defeat, the reselection issue became increasingly linked with the two other issues of constitutional reform promoted by the left, the election of the leader and the authorship of the manifesto. And as both sides of the party began to draw their battle lines, and conducted the customary post-mortem which follows loss of office, it became less and less an issue on its own merits, but a weapon in the power struggle within the party. Although the arguments in favour of reselection had won the day, and the supporters of mandatory reselection had come close to winning the vote too, the right of the party still hoped for a return to the status quo ante 1978. The agreement to set up an inquiry into all aspects of the party's organisation seemed to provide a breathing space for the moderates, led by Callaghan, but before the 1979 conference the NEC succeeded in passing, against the party leader, a resolution which waived the three-year rule so as to allow the constitutional issues to be debated again as a matter of urgency. And it was additionally agreed that whatever the conference decided, the commission of inquiry could also look at the three constitutional reforms.

When the 1979 conference met, the CLPD seemed to have achieved 'an unstoppable momentum' (*New Statesman*, 5 October 1979). Although the debate was uninspired, mandatory reselection was carried. Once again, throughout the Conference, a striking degree of hostility to the PLP was evinced by the delegates. In the reselection debate itself, Sam McCluskie of the Seamen's Union, speaking for the NEC, who was a convert to mandatory reselection, said that it could 'control the arrogance of MPs'. One speaker listed the names of those MPs whom he said had betrayed the party – these included Reg Prentice, Dick Taverne, George Brown, Richard Marsh. Another mentioned the tiny CLP memberships of some right-wing MPs; the issue was the same as it had been in 1974, 1977 and 1978, 'the right of the rank and file to have a say in whether they endorse their MPs or not'. Ian Mikardo, now in favour, said only a few supreme elitists in the PLP would oppose the new system and put this question to Callaghan:

> Do you really think that if you win today this question is going to go away and will never be raised again? . . . if these changes are not made today, they will be made next year. (For all these quotes, see Labour Party Annual Conference Report 1979, p. 262 ff.)

Reselection was carried by four million to three million, and another vote removed the usual year's delay in changes in the party's constitution so that it could be implemented immediately. NEC spokesmen made it clear, however, that the process could only happen once in the lifetime of a Parliament; indeed the conference chairman, Frank Allaun said that there would often be a short list with only one name, that of the sitting MP. This was later to become a matter of bitter argument, but in any case the status of the conference's decisions was open to question because of the party inquiry, which included the constitutional issues in its terms of reference, and they would therefore come up for debate yet again at the 1980 conference.

The inquiry did not succeed in offering a solution to the deepening crisis within the party, as some optimists had hoped it would. While it endorsed the idea of mandatory reselection, it was unable to bring forward agreed proposals on the other two constitutional issues, the control of the manifesto and the election of the leader. All that emerged was the notion of an electoral college and a determination by union leaders to reinstate the three-year rule. David Basnett, chairman of the commission, voiced their feelings when he said at the 1980 conference, 'We cannot afford to go through another period of division, acrimony and misunderstanding such as has occurred on these issues over the past two or three years' (Labour Party Annual Conference Report 1980, p. 86).

At the 1980 conference then, the three issues were debated once more, this time all in the same afternoon, allowing even less time than usual for discussion. The proposal to give the NEC the final say on the manifesto was narrowly defeated; on the leadership election, conference agreed to alter the franchise, but failed to agree on how this should be done, thus necessitating a special conference in January 1981. Mandatory reselection was voted in, by a small margin; the AUEW Engineering Section voted against for the first time. The issue had been debated for four successive years, and the debate was very short. A critical amendment proposed a return to the 1978 formula, but the feeling of the conference was very much against this. Joe Ashton – one of the very few MPs who had ever addressed the conference on this issue – was slow handclapped when he suggested, perhaps with more prescience than he realised, that mandatory reselection would be 'the biggest push to the three-party system that the political system had ever seen' (Labour Party Annual Conference Report 1980, p. 141). The unpleasant scene which took place between MPs and conference delegates marked the nadir of relations between these two sections of the party.

One new aspect came into the argument, however. A speaker who supported mandatory reselection said that reselection conferences, which would gather several potential candidates as well as the sitting MP would offer 'all GMCs and the party as a whole the opportunity to see the kind of talent that is available'. This was taken a little further by a black delegate in a short but powerful speech. He argued that the proposal would substitute democracy for elitism; the clique who currently held power in the party would have to share that power,

> And what is that clique at present? The clique is middle-class; the clique is essentially male; the clique at present is absolutely and totally white. The only way we are going to get alternative talent heard is to give them the opportunity at reselections across the country (p. 141).

Thus reselection was no longer seen as just a means of replacing an MP who had lost touch with his constituency party, but also as a political talent contest. The CLPD had previously put forward the proposal that all shortlists for parliamentary candidates should include a woman and a manual worker.

This question of the shortlist was what kept controversy alive; was a shortlist of one constitutional? A number of reselections took place where the MP was the only nominee. The NEC had laid down that any short list drawn up must include the MP's name. In addition it was open to the GMC to add names to that list at the selection conference itself, a practice which had been permitted under normal selection rules in the past. The CLPD, however, took the line that short lists of only one flouted the spirit of the decision on mandatory reselection taken at the 1980 conference. It felt indeed that it was in effect a return to the Mikardo compromise of 1978. There was particular annoyance, it was reported, over the reselection of Betty Boothroyd at West Bromwich West. The short list had consisted of her name alone, in spite of the fact that the left-wing challenger had received eight nominations and had only been prevented from going forward to the selection conference by a narrow voting margin in the executive committee. Subsequently, the NEC passed a resolution that shortlists of one should not be the normal practice where several nominations had been submitted. This was strongly opposed by moderates on the committee. One of their number, John Golding said:

> The constituency parties are absolutely within their rights to have a short list of one when they are totally satisfied with their MP. I think that the majority of the Executive (the NEC) are trying to bulldoze constituency parties out of their rights, and I deplore that (*The Times*, 28 May 1981).

After this decision, several 'token' contests took place, where CLPs anxious both to reselect their MP and also to stick to the rules, nominated another candidate merely as a matter of form.

In practice reselection has not so far proved the threat to right-wing MPs many had predicted. Indeed boundary changes are likely to remove more MPs than the reselection process. But distrust of the parliamentary party remains deep, and was again a feature of the conference in 1981. In a debate on 'Power and the PLP', the principal motion instructed the NEC 'to integrate the virtually autonomous PLP' by incorporating its standing orders into the party constitution. One speaker said that 'much of the distrust that is evident between MPs and the rest of the movement stems from what is seen as the separation of the PLP from the party'. The defection of twenty-five Labour MPs to the new Social Democratic Party – another betrayal in the long history of betrayals which the party has suffered and which contribute powerfully to its ethos – is a major factor in this distrust. One speaker at the 1981 conference mentioned this:

> In the past we have trusted people like Shirley Williams, George Brown, Reg Prentice. Where are they now? They are in the enemy camp.

Many of the defectors already had serious problems with their constituency parties and were likely to have found reselection difficult; others were threatened by boundary changes which would have affected their constituencies.

But only a small number of MPs have been replaced by their constituency parties. Some had previously had problems with their management committees. All have been replaced by someone of more left-wing views. One example is John Sever, MP for Birmingham Ladywood. He had taken over the seat in 1977 from Brian Walden, a prominent right-winger who resigned from Parliament to pursue a career in television, leaving a constituency party with a tiny membership and poor organisation. Under left-wing influence, a revival had taken place and relations with the MP had deteriorated. There were several candidates at the selection conference, including a Militant supporter, and several ballots were necessary before Albert Bore, a left-winger, was selected. The chairman of the CLP expressed the view that the party appeared to be 'less pro-Bore than against John Sever' (*Sunday Times*, 24 May and 7 June 1981).

Another MP who lost his nomination was Fred Mulley. MP for Sheffield Park. He was the loser in a political talent contest. At 63, with several heart attacks behind him, there might have been a good case for asking him to retire, though he had been a most successful MP for thirty-two years. Chosen in his place for what will be, even after boundary changes, one of the safest Labour seats in the country, was Richard Caborn, seen by many as one of the most influential politicians in the city, and its representative in the European Parliament. Caborn had ignored the NEC's request that Euro-MPs should not challenge sitting MPs. Also in Sheffield, Frank Hooley, MP for Heeley, was rejected in favour of a local councillor. Hooley had had occasional trouble with his local party, and his particular failure seemed to be that he was more interested in foreign affairs than in parish pump matters, though he was by no means a right-winger. But nor were the two newly-selected candidates in the Sheffield seats extremists. Although given sensational treatment by the press, the net result of the reselection process in all these instances was probably unexceptionable to the mainstream of Labour supporters.

Another case, that of the replacement of Bradford North MP Ben Ford by a Militant supporter, Pat Wall, has raised serious doubts; and there was controversy over his endorsement as candidate after reports of a speech which predicted bloody revolution. An inquiry into the activities of the Militant Tendency was set in train.[1] Even before Wall's selection, fears had been expressed – and these were not confined to those right-wing parliamentarians who had always opposed any increased role for the extra-parliamentary party – that the constitutional changes agreed in 1980, on reselection and the election of the leader, far from introducing greater democracy could result in Members of Parliament having little or no freedom of action, and in constituency parties becoming 'a regular intimidation agency'.[2] Some feared that control of the party would pass to an elite, less accountable than the parliamentary party, because not elected; that Labour might become a vanguard party in which all dissent was stifled.

These fears were fuelléd by various incidents after the 1980 conference. For example, in November 1980, after the principle of an electoral college had been agreed, but before its precise form had been arrived at, Michael Foot was elected leader under the old rules, by the parliamentary party alone. There was pressure on MPs to fill in their ballot papers at a GMC meeting. Some refused to do so, arguing that this was an infringement of their freedom of action. Again, in September 1981, when Denis Healey and Tony Benn were contenders for the deputy leadership of the party under the new electoral college rules, some MPs feared that they might fail to be reselected if they did not support Tony Benn, who had the overwhelming support of the constituency parties. After the detailed results were known, a 'hit list' of MPs who had not voted for Benn and were due for reselection was said to have been drawn up.

A third example is provided by the CLPD pamphlet *How to Select or Reselect your MP* (Mullin 1981). It included a list of twelve 'key' votes in the Commons since 1975 on issues ranging from the EEC to terrorism and abortion, with details of how MPs voted in each case. None of the shadow cabinet and only one member of the NEC voted in the sense favoured by CLPD in all twelve divisions. This 'moral fervour' index, and Benn's deputy leadership campaign in 1981 alienated more than a few of the Tribune Group of MPs.

Actions such as these have given weight to the criticism that the CLPD and supporters of mandatory reselection will invoke democracy to the point and only to the point at which their influence will be maximised.

---

[1]'The most striking fact about the Militant Tendency is how unsuccessful it has been – all it has to show for a decade's toil is the control of a mere half-dozen constituency Labour parties – and a reputation as the greatest enemy of parliamentary socialism' (Hugo Young, *Sunday Times*, 27 June 1982).

[2]Ostrogorski, 1969, p. 317. He alleged threats against MPs reluctant to support Irish home rule, and procedural reforms in the Commons.

And their willingness to work with factions that oppose parliamentary democracy must reflect poorly on the campaign: 'Utopians who make tactical arrangements with the intolerant and the intimidatory help to legitimise them' (Kogans, 1982, p. 76). On the other hand, the reselection campaign, however carefully orchestrated, could not have succeeded without the support of many loyal but disenchanted grassroots Labour Party members, disillusioned with the experience of Labour Governments in the 1960s and 1970s. The constitutional reforms in the party have also belatedly awakened the right wing to the need for greater accountability in the party. Their reaction to the 'democracy of the committed', and the possibility of further extending democracy in the party which might satisfy MPs and party members alike, will be discussed in Chapter 10.

9 Reselection and the theory of party government

Mandatory reselection of MPs is now part of the constitution of the Labour Party. In assessing its implications, a complex web of interlocking controversies about current British politics and about contemporary attitudes to representation must be explored. The demand by Labour Party activists for greater control over Members of Parliament was, as preceding chapters have shown, a reaction to the experience of a prolonged period of Labour government at a time when 'Keynesian welfare capitalism' was breaking down, and Britain's economic problems were becoming more acute. Labour governments, under the pressure of international economic conditions combined with industrial militancy at home, appeared to the left of the party to have broken with their natural supporters, the working class. The call for mandatory reselection was a reaction against the refusal of the Wilson and Callaghan Governments to take note of the party conference, but at the same time it was a reassertion of the 1918 constitution, of the concept of the class party, and the concept of intra-party democracy, and as such it was the continuation of a struggle within the party which has never really ceased, though it may at times have seemed to be in abeyance. In the 1970s and early 1980s, as in earlier years, it was a struggle about policy, as much as about the party's constitution; here it is worth recalling Miliband's comment on the situation in the party in 1902, quoted earlier:

> Underlying the tension between activists and parliamentarians was the former fear that the Labour group in Parliament would, if it were not strictly controlled, backslide into opportunism, manoeuvre and compromise, and the latter's easy assumption that manoeuvre and compromise were inherent in their situation and essential to the furtherance of Labour's immediate aims.

This judgement remains true, but in focusing initially on the reselection of MPs, the campaign not only provoked a debate on power in the Labour Party, but also highlighted the confusion about the proper role of Members of Parliament. Along with other developments of recent years, the campaign has re-emphasised the fact that we no longer live in Burke's world, but it has also underlined the problems intrinsic in Labour's alternative theory of representation. The argument over reselection has shown up the extent of the mistrust that exists between the party's MPs and its grassroots activists; indeed it has contributed to that mistrust. It has also revealed once more the division in the party between populists and elitists. The reaction of the right of the party to the demand for greater constituency control was for a long time to deny its legitimacy – Harold Wilson's 'Samurai' speech was an example of this – or to hope that it would simply go away, as Ian Mikardo pointed out so bluntly at the 1980 Conference. Somewhat belatedly, the right became converted to the idea of party democracy; raising the fear of the excessive power of the caucus, they promoted the idea of 'one member, one vote', so as to prevent the power of reselection being in the hands of the activists alone. Thus each side favoured the definition of democracy which would benefit its own views on policy and on where power should lie in the party.

These are the themes that will be explored in this chapter and the next. But the debate, as shown in Chapter 1, was taking place against a background of rapid changes in the wider political system. General dissatisfaction with the two-party system and with adversary politics became increasingly evident, and Labour's electoral support in particular began to seem shaky. With Parliament less and less the centre of decision-making in government, the whole idea of representative government was less powerful than it had been in the past, and resort was more frequently made to forceful protest. The distance between the representatives and those they were supposed to represent seemed at times to be becoming dangerously wide, and an increasing number of commentators saw the need for reforms which would bring the political system up to date, that it might better serve the needs of the electorate.

That the demand for automatic reselection was in reaction to the events that had taken place during 1966–70 and 1974–9 showed up in the conference debates quoted from at length in earlier chapters. It was also made abundantly clear in the introduction to the CLPD pamphlet, *How to Select or Reselect Your MP* (Mullin, 1981). This rehearses the grievances of those in the party who felt that the experience of Labour governments since 1964 represented a betrayal of the party's programmes:

> After the election defeat [of 1970] most party members and many parliamentary leaders vowed that no Labour government would ever again pursue such an ignominious course (p. 4).

During the time in opposition, an industrial strategy was evolved:

> Once in office, the 1974–9 Labour government jettisoned these policies with record speed. This time, without even waiting for the

inevitable sterling crisis, they made planning agreements volun-
tary... in 1976 the government surrendered to calls by the International Monetary Fund for cuts in public spending, and unemployment more than doubled. The manifesto commitment to achieve a
fundamental change in the balance of wealth and power in favour of
working people and their families was forgotten. By the time Labour
left office, the gap between rich and poor was as wide as it had ever
been and the Labour government had again turned on its supporters
by trying to impose a 5 per cent wage limit. By the end Labour were
pursuing policies that not even a Liberal government would adopt
(pp. 4–5).

But while it was a reaction to events in the immediate past, the campaign
to exert greater control over MPs was also a harking back to the earliest
days of the party, when MPs were more clearly seen as the servants of the
movement, and when the party was the party of the workers. Class was an
indispensable element of the theory of party government which postulated
a programme which was democratically arrived at by the mass membership at the conference, presented to the electorate, and then passed into
law by the party's parliamentary representatives. Every aspect of this
theory – the notion of a class party, the idea of a mandate, intra-party
democracy, even the commitment to purely parliamentary methods – have
already at one time or another been subjected to attack, but the problems
they raise have recently been highlighted once more by the attempt to
secure greater democracy within the party.

Although the party was founded with the explicit aim of representing
the working class, once Labour had chosen the parliamentary road, and
had decided to bid for power, to become a governing party, the class
consciousness of the parliamentarians was weakened. This was a process
which started early; the first Labour MPs were soon educated in the
niceties of parliamentary politics and the slow pace of change:

> the very act of going to Parliament, of living the life of an MP with a
> middle-class salary, a secretary and all the other accoutrements of
> parliamentary life means that the MP lives in a middle-class world in
> a middle-class way ... the very business of being elected to represent
> working-class interests takes an MP out of the world he is meant to re-
> present and into the camp of the enemy. (Drucker, 1979, p. 94.)

Such a development might be to a certain extent inevitable; but in the
revisionist years, Labour was *deliberately* emptied of its working-class
content by the leadership. Gaitskell and Wilson looked forward to a classless society and the party 'succumbed to the argument of its opponents
that any attempt to mobilise an electorate on class lines is both illegitimate
and doomed to failure' (Miliband, 1961, p. 132). Gaitskell tried to deny

that Labour was a class party and in the same breath charged the Conservatives with the same offence.[1] Wilson, like MacDonald before him, was Prime Minister at a time when the country was beset by economic problems, and keen to prove, to national and international financial institutions particularly, Labour's 'fitness to govern'. This, added to a desire to appeal to the maximum number of voters, led to even greater insistence on a 'classless' image for the party.

The end of post-war prosperity, and of consensus politics, and the rise of unemployment have made it easier for the left of the party to revive the class issue, and it is one which has played an important part in the reselection campaign, as conference speeches quoted earlier have shown. Since 1945 the parliamentary party has become progressively more 'middle class', both in terms of education and of occupation. Manual workers, a majority in the PLP in the inter-war years, are now only a small percentage of the group. This change is still more marked in the composition of the cabinet and shadow cabinet.

Distrust of the leadership has always been a characteristic of Labour Party members – a part of the defensive working-class ethos – and this distrust has over recent years come to embrace much of the parliamentary party; there is an 'empathic gap' (Minkin, 1974) as well as a gap on policy between the leadership, dominated by university-educated professionals, and the membership, still largely composed of manual workers. Another, less sympathetic writer, has criticised this view as 'cultural and emotional proletarianism'. But Labour's class identity is more than merely an emotional attitude; it has important political consequences, for the PLP as well as the rest of the party. One left-wing trade unionist, later elected to Parliament himself, expressed this clearly as long ago as 1972, at a time when reselection was not the burning issue within the party which it was later to become; arguing that CLPs should not shrink from sacking their MPs, he urged the selection of 'good working-class candidates instead of professional politicians as the only way to alter the middle-class character of the PLP and make it more representative of the party as a whole' (Roberts, 1972). The view has important implications for representative theory. One of its strongest exponents is Dennis Skinner:

[1]"Somehow we let the Tories get away with the monstrous falsehood that we are a class party and they are not'. (Quoted in Miliband, 1961, p. 347.) This question is not unique to the Labour party. Socialist parties in other European countries, France especially, have faced similar problems about control of their representatives, and class has been an important factor (see Duverger, 1964, pp. 191 ff). Duverger quotes an apposite remark by Robert de Jouvenel: 'Two deputies from different parties have more in common than a deputy and a militant member of the same party' (pp. 201–2).

We want these people [MPs] to represent their class interest and not this bogus national interest we hear so much about. I want people in Parliament who are dedicated to carrying out that class interest (*The Times*, 29 September 1980).

On another occasion, he returned to the same subject. An MP's role is limited, he argued; because of the class divisions within society, he cannot represent all his constituents, and it is a fatal mistake to think otherwise. He must know what the grassroots are thinking and 'take the election-night spirit to Westminster' (speech at Sheffield University, 27 February 1981).

Although this class-based view fits into the Labour theory of party government, and with the idea of MPs as delegates of their local parties, and with the theory of the mandate, it is at odds with the essentially individualistic liberal theory of the constitution and Burke's definition of the role of an MP, both of which still have an enduring hold. Nor has it found a ready response in the majority of the parliamentary party. Speaking after the SDP victory at the Hillhead by-election in April 1982, Peter Shore attacked this perception of class relationships; too many in the party, he said, saw Britain as having a structure in which the majority was still denied all rights and was oppressed by a ruling class. Such a view may have been appropriate in the 1840s or even the 1920s, but it ignored the vast improvements since the Second World War, achievements of Labour governments and of organised labour (*The Times*, 29 March 1982).

What is more, this view is in contradiction to the views of the voters as a whole, and to the increasingly complex nature of modern society. In a country in which differences based on nationality, language or religion have not gained political significance, 'class differences predominate by default' (Richard Rose, 1976, p. 43); but social class is no longer such a sure guide to voting behaviour as it once was: as many working-class votes may be cast for Conservatives as for Labour. Only a fifth of the electorate conform to class stereotypes; as few as 9 per cent of voters are archetypal manual workers, and only 12 per cent pure middle-class types (Richard Rose, 1976, pp. 41–2). In these circumstances, not surprisingly, fewer voters than in the past are prepared to identify themselves with a class; less than half the electorate in October in 1974 would identify themselves with their 'natural' class party. (See Crewe *et al.*, 1977.) The attempts by the two main parties to revive class politics have had a lukewarm reception from the electorate, as voting figures at successive general elections have shown.

Closely related both to the class issue and to the distrust of the party's elected representatives in Parliament is the question – now controversial once more – of the role that direct action should play in Labour politics. The early Labour Party inherited a long tradition of working-class politics

which favoured gradual reform and rejected violent revolution. Hostile to
the politics of other left-wing groups such as the Communist Party,
Labour placed 'all its faith in the reforming potential of the Parliamentary
State' (David Coates, 1975, p. 25). It has believed in the essential neutral-
ity of the state and with a few exceptions has opposed the use of industrial
power to support political demands. But in the late 1960s and early 1970s,
a growing disillusionment with normal political channels became clear;
extra-parliamentary action of all kinds became more frequent. Pressure
groups were willing to use more open forms of pressure, and demon-
strations and sit-ins became common. The Labour movement, too, moved
onto the street. Opposition to the Heath Government's Industrial
Relations Act, and the campaign against the 1972 Housing Finance Act
and the subsequent Clay Cross affair illustrated a feeling in some quarters
that parliamentary action was not enough. This feeling was not shared by
the parliamentary leadership and the majority of the PLP. The first
general election of 1974 was called on the issue of direct action; Heath's
defeat took place outside Parliament. The experience of that government
led many on the left to the conclusion that there was a need for an 'extra-
parliamentary dimension', believing that all radical change comes from
outside. Those on the left of the party who had never really believed in the
possibility of socialism by parliamentary means were strengthened in their
belief by the experience of successive Labour governments being 'blown
off course'. The whole notion of the parliamentary method was based on
the belief that, once in power, Labour would be able to make fundamental
changes in society. The failure, as the left saw it, of Labour governments
to achieve this, led to a disillusionment in some quarters with parliamentary government and to an increased stress on direct action.

Robin Blackburn probably voiced the opinions of many of those who
held such views when he wrote that Labour is too involved with 'the
establishment'. 'The real dividing line between social democrats and revolutionaries', he continued, 'is their attitude towards Parliament and the
bourgeois state machine it inhabits' ('Labour and the Marxist Left', *New
Statesman*, 14 September 1973). He argued that there was a need to
develop an alternative to the Labour leadership, a united front of socialists. The development of such a movement and some of its views have
been traced by another left-wing writer:

> The current Labour left, unlike any before it, is not simply or even
> mainly a parliamentary force...[it] captured control of the party
> conference by mobilising an alliance between left MPs, constituency
> activists, and crucially, the votes of the delegations from the big trade
> unions. For the first time, some of the Labour left activists in Parlia-
> ment and in the constituencies established a firm organisational
> connection, through their alliance with the leaders of the large

unions, with the groundswell of working-class industrial militancy. (David Coates, 1975, p. 209.)

The development of such an alliance and the growth of such attitudes in the party served to emphasise the division in the party between the leadership and the right of the parliamentary party on the one hand, and the increasingly assertive left on the other. The distaste of many MPs for the stress on the class origins of the party, their refusal to countenance direct action, and their fear of the growing strength of the left at conference and in the CLPs, contributed to their opposition to the campaign by CLPD for greater democracy in the party.

It was basically a conflict between elitists and populists. The elitists generally thought they knew 'what was in the interests of everyone, or almost everyone' (Richard Rose, 1976, p. 297). The populists were chiefly concerned with the interest of the mass of the relatively uneducated and unwealthy, regarding most working-class demands as legitimate. This division in the party was probably at its most obvious on the Common Market issue; the possibility of British entry aroused the populists' fears of a foreign, capitalist, elitist club. It was supported by those in the party who were most middle-class, and who could readily be portrayed as arrogant. Their anti-majoritarian stance was open to easy attack. As one MP said in the 1971 debate 'What is the point of having MPs who do not do what the people want?' The same kind of feeling has often been evident in the argument over reselection, the election of the leader and the manifesto. The populist/elitist conflict has also been at the centre of disputes between MPs and their constituency parties. One of the causes of the antagonism between Taverne and the leaders of his local party was his opposition to direct action against the Industrial Relations Act. Similarly, Sandelson and his CLP disagreed over the issue of the Shrewsbury pickets. Powerful anti-elitist and anti-MP attitudes have been voiced at successive Labour Party Conferences. What is the point, party activists have asked, of having MPs who do not share their views?

The link between the party's representatives in Parliament and the mass membership, in particular the active membership, is the party programme. The idea of a legislative programme, as so much else in this debate, has its origins far back in history (see Beer, 1965, p. 6), but it was not until the end of the nineteenth century, when the Liberal Party was at the height of its powers, that the concept of a mandate for a particular programme gained ground; the Conservative Party at the time was reluctant to accept this approach. In the twentieth century, however, with the rise of the Labour Party, the mandate has come to play a major part in electoral politics, and in the justification of government, by whichever party. The voters have a choice at general elections between two distinct programmes put forward by opposing political parties. The successful party is then committed to carrying out its programme and the party's MPs are committed to supporting it. The MP is mandated, 'but this is not a local mandate. Party has distilled the interests and aspirations of a class into a comprehensive social philosophy' (Beer, 1965, p. 87); belonging rather than agreement is the basis of party allegiance. This approach to government has been basic to the Labour Party since its foundation. It embodies old trade union traditions about the mandating of delegates and the policy-making powers of a conference. Its correlative is intra-party democracy.

Clement Attlee expressed the theory in these words:

> The candidate of one of the major parties stands for a connected policy and for a certain body of men, who, if a majority can be obtained, will form a Government. This is well understood by the electors. If the Member fails to support the Government or fails to act with the Opposition in their efforts to turn the Government out, he is acting contrary to the expectation of those who have put their trust in him. (Quoted in Beer, 1965, p. 87.)

But 'manifestoism' has come to mean far more than what is implied in this statement. It has also been taken over by the Conservative Party and has become a major feature of electoral strategy for all political parties. The idea of a programme has come to mean much more than just a 'connected policy'. Between 1945 and 1974, Conservative manifestos doubled in length, and Labour's grew by a factor of three. While the policy exercise carried out for the Conservative Party by R. A. Butler after 1945 involved three committees and confined itself to sketching broad themes, Edward Heath in the late 1960s had thirty committees and went into great detail on specific items of policy. Similarly, in the Labour Party, a vast amount of work went into preparing the manifestos, especially that for the 1979 election, and there is now a 'rolling' manifesto, which covers more than 200 pages. Pledges made by the parties were correspondingly increased in number. By 1974, both parties, who had made pledges on a dozen issues or less in 1900, were committing themselves in more than seventy different and specific ways.

There is no doubt that the parties attach considerable importance to these election pledges; the civil service, too, pays a great deal of attention to them. The fact that they are a constraint on governments has been made clear on several occasions by members of the Thatcher government. Mrs Thatcher herself has continually referred to the manifesto, and her Chancellor of the Exchequer, Sir Geoffrey Howe, has been quoted as saying to a party committee, that he was hemmed in by election pledges which reduced his room for manoeuvre – 'there are road blocks all around me', he has said (*The Times*, 26 November 1980). But manifesto commitments can also be used as a justification for carrying out a particular policy, either in the face of public opposition or presumably as a weapon against bureaucratic reluctance. Mrs Thatcher told the 1979 Conservative conference:

> Those who voted Conservative know the principles we stand for. We have every right to carry them out and we shall.

The newly formed Social Democratic Party will also have a party programme to which its MPs will be committed:

> MPs will be required to have full regard to the election programme and adopt statements of the SDP but will not be mandated nor subject to the direction or control of any organ of the party. (*The Times*, 23 September 1981).

Nor is this exclusively a British phenomenon; François Mitterrand, not long after his election to the French Presidency, declared 'Frenchmen and women can note that what was promised is being carried out, without anything being added or subtracted', thus going rather further than British politicians have done.

The idea of a mandate for a programme is, however, open to a variety of criticisms, both as a theory of government and as a representative mechanism. From the point of view of a government the most obvious difficulty is that no matter how much importance the party leadership and even the cabinet itself may attach to a particular commitment, or series of commitments, other considerations, political and economic, national and international, may force them to abandon it. A government, whatever its political colour, 'has to cope with a moving escalator of national and international events' (David Wood, *The Times*, 7 July 1980), which may prevent it from carrying out its promises. The most obvious example of this is the public expenditure cuts forced on the Labour government in 1976 by the International Monetary Fund; but there are also cases in which the Government's own back-benchers have been the cause of a failure to fulfil a pledge – for instance on devolution to Scotland and Wales in 1979. Such constraints are bound to operate whatever the complexion of the bureaucracy; no manifesto can be a complete guide to the future.

Doubt is cast on manifestoism not only by the necessities of governing, but also by the effect on electoral choice. Extensive research has shown that the contents of a party's programme are not a strong influence on voting. But by supporting a particular party, the voter is willy-nilly supporting a programme, some elements of which he may not agree with, and for which the party, if successful in the election, will claim a mandate, as Mrs Thatcher's remarks quoted above show only too clearly. As one critic trenchantly put it: 'Mandates for shopping lists of 60–80 specific items are without meaning' (Finer, 1975b).

A further criticism is this: the manifesto idea is based on a two-party system, two distinct classes with distinct programmes between which the voter may choose. The breakdown of class/party alignment has already been mentioned, but there is another problem in present circumstances, where the two-party system seems to be rapidly fragmenting, and electoral support for the winning party, even if it has a clear majority of parliamentary seats, is being eroded. Can it really make sense for a party to claim a mandate where almost 60 per cent of the popular vote has been cast elsewhere, as happened in May 1979? Yet Lord Thorneycroft claimed a 'great mandate'. One may go further than this; the theory assumes not only a two-party system, but one-party government. This is no longer as assured as it was in the past, as Callaghan's being obliged to rely on Liberal support in 1977–8 made clear. It is therefore no longer the case that the voter 'knows that the victorious party will surely be able to carry out the programme to which it is pledged' (Beer, 1965, p. 87). What is more, if – as is entirely possible – the new SDP–Liberal Alliance gains a sizeable block of parliamentary seats at the next general election, a co-alition government might be formed. In such circumstances, manifesto pledges would be likely to become bargaining counters in a complex game of parliamentary wheeling and dealing.

These are general criticisms of the mandate theory, but for the Labour Party, the programme is much more than an electoral ploy. It is in theory also a reflection of the ideas and wishes of the party membership voiced at the party conference: 'The decisive will and main thrust of ideas must come from the rank and file' (Beer, 1965, p. 88). The manifesto is thus written for a multiple audience, which includes the converted as well as those the party would hope to convert. It is also, frequently, in spite of the preparatory work, written in a great hurry, and under pressure to unite the party before the coming election. In 1970, for instance, 'the controversial policy items were smoothed over . . . stated in non-committal terms or simply avoided entirely' (Minkin, 1978, p. 313). In 1979, Callaghan refused to allow the inclusion in the manifesto of several policy items that had been voted as part of the party programme by the annual conference. The most notable, because the most emotive, item was abolition of the House of Lords, and Callaghan was later subjected to bitter attacks for having ignored the conference. The post-1979 inquest proved the truth of the dictum that manifestoism is 'an attempt to control Labour's barely trusted leaders' (Drucker, 1979, p. 93).

If recent experience has devalued the mandate theory, it has also thrown doubt on the concept of intra-party democracy. This, as Samuel Beer pointed out, derives 'from a deep strain of democratic theory', but it has been strenuously attacked, both by some Labour parliamentarians, and by academic commentators, notably the late Robert McKenzie. The attack has two main strands: that intra-party democracy is contrary to British political tradition, which holds that those who make national policy should be free of commitments, and that its exercise gives power to extremists.

The first argument tends to lose its force when it is recalled that any contemporary government, of whatever party, has commitments of all kinds to which it is bound to pay regard, to a whole range of pressure groups, to organised business and organised labour, as well as its extra-parliamentary party. The Conservative Party today, even if its conference has less power than that of the Labour Party, is no less committed to a clear set of policies, even to a comprehensive social philosophy. The Tribune pamphlet (Allaun *et al.*, 1972) made the point rather well: 'The fatal weakness of this argument is that it is applied only to the relationship between a Labour Government and its own party members.'

On the other hand, it is clear that the feeling expressed at most party conferences since 1970, and especially recently, *has* increasingly favoured curtailing the flexibility of a Labour government. The most telling argument against this is that government cannot consist merely in putting into effect pre-decided policies – the 'moving staircase' argument. But Labour Governments have often refused to concede anything at all to the conference. Harold Wilson refused to accept a resolution at the 1970 conference which said 'while appreciating that the PLP must deal with matters arising in Parliament which have not been the subject of annual conference decision, it deplored the PLP's refusal to act on conference decisions'. As Miliband (1958) replied to McKenzie, the leadership has always had a wide margin when in office, and even if the leadership always has the last word, intra-party democracy at least ensures that there is a dialogue. In the Wilson years, this dialogue seemed at times to have ceased. On many occasions, the leadership seemed to the activists not only to have had the last word, but to have treated them with contempt.

The second line of argument against intra-party democracy is that it puts power over policy into the hands of a few who are likely, by virtue of their activism, to be extremists. This is not a new view, as previous references to Ostrogorski have shown; Sidney Webb called activists 'a bunch of cranks and fanatics'. Much has been made of this idea by those opposed to mandatory reselection, but though the apparent increase in the influence of the Militant Tendency does give cause for concern, Richard Rose's findings, quoted in Chapter 1, do not support the idea that activists are necessarily extremists, in spite of the evidence on the policy preferences of Labour voters being out of tune with those of many active party members.

More than this, to deny party democracy by curtailing the policy-making role of the conference, or indeed by abolishing the new rules for reselection, as some on the right of the party might like to do, would not improve Labour's claim to be a democratic party. Nor would it help to re-vitalise the party or to improve membership, both necessary if the party is to regain its electoral strength. The arguments in favour of grassroots participation in policy-making and in the choice of leaders must today be powerful ones for these reasons. Indeed, they are now apparently accepted by two former Labour ministers, David Owen and Shirley Williams, who both in recent books (Owen, 1981, Williams, 1981) attacked the concepts of party democracy, as stifling argument and promoting party government over parliamentary government. Yet they are now part of the leadership of the SDP; the draft constitution of this new party would commit it (and them) to rank and file participation in policy-making and the choice of rep-resentatives at every level.

The real heart of the matter is the ramshackle nature of Labour's democracy. What is necessary is an overall improvement in the democratic system of the party, which could bring together the various sections of the party – PLP, activists and members. The composition of Labour's confer-ence and the voting methods used are hardly democratic. In particular, there is the question of the block vote of the trade unions. With the fall in the individual membership of the party and the rise in affiliated member-ship through the unions, conference decisions are now more than ever made by the block vote. MPs and candidates have no vote at conference unless they are CLP delegates, and recent events have shown up the fact that small cliques can swing conference votes. The block vote is clearly an unsatisfactory mechanism when a large union such as the AUEW has nearly twice the votes of all the constituency parties put together. As is often pointed out, the block vote is merely customary, not constitutional. In the USA, the Democratic Party abolished it for Presidential con-ventions in 1972, on the grounds that it encouraged 'boss rule', and Minkin has shed fascinating light on the operations of 'Carron's Law' at Labour conferences in the 1950s and early 1960s. Strenuous politicking behind the scenes usually led to Bill Carron, leader of the AEU, having his own way, often in the face of fierce objections from the rest of the union's delegation. But

> if the union's position was still in doubt at the end of the conference debate, Carron had the supreme advantage over those who sought to democratise the decision – *he* carried the card (Minkin, 1978, p. 186).

Votes at more recent conferences have proved again the truth of Robert McKenzie's old gibe about stage armies.

Abolition of the block vote would not reduce the power of the unions; rather it would disperse it, thus permitting more room for the smaller unions and the constituency parties to make their views felt. In addition to the voting arrangements, the principles on which many unions are run, though sometimes superficially democratic, are often the opposite. Some union leaders are elected for life. One MP, criticising the electoral college proposals, said 'Some of these guys make the Politburo look liberal.' (Tom Litterick, *The Times*, 29 September 1980.)

There is also a case for altering the composition of the National Executive Committee. The separation between the parliamentary party and the party in the country has been one of the themes of this study; so too has the gulf between the Labour activists and Labour voters. Closer links between these elected bodies and their respective electors could be of great use in uniting the party. As at conference, the parliamentary party is not represented on the NEC; MPs are only on the committee if they are elected by one of the three sections of the committee, representing trade unions, constituency parties and women. The constituency section was created in 1937, after a campaign for rank and file representation, and has always consisted of MPs or former MPs who have been unrepresentative of the PLP as a whole. Since 1951, it has been, with the exceptions of Healey and Callaghan, 'a Bevanite, unilateralist, Clause Fourist, anti-marketeer, Tribunite closed shop' (Ben Pimlott, *New Statesman*, 23 September 1977). Representation of the PLP *per se* on the NEC could go some way to closing the gap which is so detrimental to the party.

Those who have opposed intra-party democracy have tried to portray it as a threat to parliamentary government, tried to tar with the Militant brush all left-wingers who favour an extension of power to the party activists. This is unfair: though there has been a discernible impatience with and mistrust of parliamentary government – an impatience which has not been confined to the Labour Party – there are also many on the left who value Parliament and its institutions. One of these is Ken Coates. Arguing that small factions such as the Workers' Revolutionary Party are too small and too divorced from the real political concerns of working people to be influential, he says that socialists must not ignore Parliament, 'for all the powers which have seeped away from it, it is a focal point of continuing importance' (1973). Indeed it can be argued that ignoring the demands for intra-party democracy will only give strength to the anti-parliamentary left.

On the other hand, the left have sought to restrict the extension of party democracy to a small group of activists in each constituency; and the oligarchical electoral college is only elitism with a different face. Another left-winger who has written scathing critiques of the Wilson and Callaghan governments, concludes in his most recent work *Labour in Power?* that 'socialist left must value and defend those [liberal democratic] political institutions. . . . Indeed, the equation of socialism with democracy is vital, for a socialist society that is not democratic is not worth having' (David Coates, 1980, pp. 282–3). If Labour is to call itself democratic, it must provide the opportunity for the expression of a wider range of views. Only thus can the gulf between ordinary people and active party members be bridged.

10 Reselection: the opportunity to involve all party members

Chapter 9 discussed some of the inadequacies of the Labour theory of representation. This final chapter will deal more specifically with the role of MPs and their relations with their local parties. Labour MPs, through the reselection process, are now more accountable than ever before, but, as already suggested, this accountability will be worth little if it is only to a tiny group. A democracy in which few participate is an empty one. Some of those who oppose the new reselection rules have argued that an MP should only be accountable to the electorate; this view relies too much on Burke to have much relevance today. As Roy Hattersley wrote about his own reselection:

> The single promise of unfettered judgement, used honestly and objectively as the Member – and only the Member – thinks best, was the product of a less educated and more deferential age. In the era of party manifestos and party whips, it is a romantic fiction (*The Times*, 14 July 1981).

Parties are here to stay; they have become an indispensable part of the representative system. But the changes that have taken place in British government and politics over the last fifteen years mean that party government no longer performs so well the representative functions which are claimed for it. The electorate, to whom the MP is ultimately responsible, do not turn out so readily at elections, and more seats are won on a minority vote. As many studies have shown, people vote for the party not the man, but there seems to be a growing gulf between the parties and what they stand for, and what the electorate wants. Reforms of all kinds are proposed to remedy this situation; these include increased use of the referendum, primary elections and the introduction of proportional representation. Such proposals are methods of bringing more people into the process of political argument and political choice. This chapter will argue that reselection could make a modest contribution to this, if the rules were changed so as to involve all the party membership.

Mandatory reselection is intended to increase MPs' accountability to their local parties. Party coherence has always been the result, not only of party discipline within Parliament, but also of the fact that local parties are generally dominated by people who insist that MPs adhere to national party policies. As Attlee's formulation of the theory of party government made clear, if an MP fails to act with his party, 'he is acting contrary to the expectation of those who put their trust in him'. The Taverne case was an example of this formula being put into practice, and indeed with the relaxation of parliamentary discipline, which benefited the pro-Marketeers as well as the left-wing rebels, it could be argued that the constituency party was the only check on Taverne's actions. Some of the other sixty-eight who voted with the Conservatives in October 1971 did have problems with their local parties. For some it became a source of long-lasting animosity, but none lost his seat. In general, however, the disputes between MPs and their local parties were not a result of failing to support the party in Parliament. Increasingly in the Wilson years, some local parties expected their MP *not* to support the government, even to vote against it. The Attlee formula is thus too simple. When the party is split between the leadership and the activists, parliamentary discipline cannot be maintained, and 'the conference decision may not command PLP obedience, but it can protect the dissident MP from party expulsion and the denial of candidature' (Minkin, 1978, p. 310).

Thus the tables were in a sense turned, and it was the loyal MP who supported the party faithfully in the Commons who found himself in some cases in trouble with his local party. In these circumstances, neither Burke nor the theory of party government can provide a defence; the situation is too complex. It may be more to the point, then, to examine the other side of the argument:

> There is no warrant in sense or logic for the idea that he [the MP] may behave as he chooses, change his views at will, get blithely out of touch with the people on whose canvassing efforts he relied, and still reckon on term after term as candidate and MP. (*New Statesman*, editorial, 16 September 1977.)

Earlier chapters have shown the course of the reselection campaign and indicated its causes. Above all, what emerges from the experience of the last twelve or fifteen years is that the Labour Party is divided between the party in Parliament and the party in the country.

The view of a former Labour MP, now in the SDP, is also worth quoting:

> parties belong to their members. It is because the Labour right forgot that and tried to keep control of their party through clever backstairs manipulation, rather than through honest argument honestly put, that the Bennite left is now making the running at conference, in the

National Executive and in most constituencies. (D. Marquand, *London Review of Books*, 1–14 October 1981.)

There is no doubt that some MPs did get out of touch with their constituencies; some were never in touch. As J. S. Mill saw so long before, the MP who 'grows cool to the interests of those who choose him' is bound to create resentment in the constituency, and especially in the local party, his power base. Any MP who can refer to his GMC as 'half wits' as Sandelson did, is not only showing contempt for those who had worked and canvassed on his behalf, but courting dismissal. Other MPs have not been so openly rude and arrogant, but they neglected their constituencies and their local parties, and appeared oblivious to the new mood in the Labour Party. Ignoring it rather than facing up to it, as Harold Wilson found in his relations with the party conference, is not a successful answer to the problem.

It was such cases which gave strength to the arguments of the Campaign for Labour Party Democracy. Its pamphlet *How to Select or Reselect Your MP* includes a section entitled 'working together':

> The purpose of mandatory reselection is to establish an honest and open relationship between the MP and his or her constituency party in the hope that, whatever the practicalities of office, our representatives in Parliament are never again allowed to lose sight of the ideals of the movement which sent them there.
> Such a relationship cannot develop overnight. The habit of consultation between an MP and his or her constituency party will only be gradually acquired and it will depend as much upon the enthusiasm of party members as upon the MP.

In order to achieve his cooperation, the local party must have information about what the MP is saying and doing. This would involve knowledge of how he voted, in PLP and NEC meetings. Votes in the Commons are, of course, public knowledge, but today so many important votes are taken in party meetings that this seems a fairly natural extension. The pamphlet goes on to ask that MPs should report back fully to their General Management Committees and consult with them on important issues.

These ideas have been vehemently attacked. Such a strengthening of party control, it is argued, would reduce MPs to mere rubber stamps, and if they failed to toe the party line, they would lose their jobs. Indeed they might even face the dilemma of being 'torn between obeying the Whips and keeping a Labour government in power or disobeying the Whips and keeping their seats' (Shirley Williams, *Guardian*, 9 July 1979). Against this, it makes no sense to claim a kind of freehold. Burke himself certainly did not. Even if some of the left do wish to bind MPs hand and foot, this does not mean that reselection provisions themselves or the ideas advanced in the pamphlet above are necessarily a grave threat to MPs. Some MPs do consult closely with their local management committees, and as Roy Hattersley commented on his own reselection:

> A Labour MP who tells his local party to mind its own business is in the wrong business himself.

Although it has become a weapon in the battle between left and right in the party, mandatory reselection could provide an opportunity to bridge the gap between the PLP, the activists and the ordinary party members. It could contribute to a revival of activity at grassroots level, and improve recruitment. As Hodgson points out in his recent study, *Labour at the Crossroads*, reselection is 'the only structured link between the CLPs and the Labour MPs in Parliament after the original selection of the parliamentary candidate' (1981, p. 37).

Without the efforts of the CLP – which selects him in the first place – and the voters who voted for him, the MP would not have his Westminster seat. There is much to be said for strengthening those links, not only with the activists, but also with the ordinary party members. Though the experience of reselection so far does not justify the fears it aroused – it has not notably favoured the 'whizz kids' as Joe Ashton predicted, nor have large numbers of MPs lost their candidatures – the arrangements for re-selection, as they are presently constituted, ignore the ordinary party members.

The power of selection and reselection is in the hands of General Management Committees, and they guard that power jealously. Only some of the membership of these committees is really active, attending most meetings and working hard at other tasks in the constituency. Not surprisingly, these people feel that they are in some special sense the party (see Finer, 1980, p. 120): their role is a basic one. And they feel that their reward for canvassing and addressing envelopes should be the selection and reselection of the candidate – what Finer calls 'Doorknocker democracy'. Left-wingers have not only resisted the idea of diffusing power to the whole membership, but have argued that only those GMC members who have attended a certain proportion of meetings should be entitled to vote at selection conferences. The Tribune pamphlet put this view:

> In most CLPs the regular attenders are only a fraction of the GMC membership. When there is a selection conference, the whole membership is liable to turn up and swamp the regular activists.

To prevent this, it would further have restricted those entitled to take part in selections; and in 1978, the constituency party rules were altered so as to restrict attendance on such occasions to those who had been present at at least one meeting in the preceding twelve months. Those who devote most of their leisure hours to the party have little time for those who only turn up to occasional meetings and are preoccupied with minor local issues. If they have not done their share of the party's chores, it is felt, they should not be allowed to choose the candidate.

It is also said that only GMC members have the skill necessary for selecting a candidate; but another, perhaps more basic, reason for opposing the involvement of the whole membership – 'a dilution of democracy' as one left-winger called it (Wise, 1979) – is that they fear the influence of the press and other media, so often hostile to left-wing views. One response to the one-man, one-vote idea was this:

> We must be on our guard against these moves . . . it would be a way of letting our enemies take over. (*The Times*, 2 March 1980.)

The left therefore prefer the current method of reselection by the GMC. The ordinary members can vote for a delegate to the committee, and can also nominate candidates through their wards or union branches. But when it meets as a reselection conference, the GMC is a group of individuals who make personal choices, they are not delegates, and the ordinary members may not be consulted at all. There have been cases, as in the Gower constituency, where the selection of a candidate has gone against the wishes even of the GMC; the executive committee, which makes up the shortlist, failed to include on it two nominees who had received the most nominations from wards and union branches (*The Times*, 24 March 1981). More recently, at Hemel Hempstead, the GMC selected a candidate against the wishes of most ward members (*The Times*, 24 June 1982). Nor do party activities do much to improve the cohesion between activists, members and voters. The GMC is a minority chosen by a minority, and 'there is no institutionalised means by which the CLP leaders can determine the views of their traditional supporters, especially on national policy' (Janosik, 1968, p. 60). There is little opportunity for contact with ordinary voters; the impact of the mass media as a means of education on political matters has been overestimated, and the party's own role in political education has been neglected (Seyd and Minkin, 1979, pp. 613–15).[1]

The arguments in favour of opening up the selection process to a wider group are made stronger by the fact that the party's membership has fallen to its lowest level for fifty years. The small number of activists take on the character of a 'Calvinist elect' (Bogdanor, 1981, p. 115), isolated from the

---

[1] *The Times* reported on 9 February 1981 that only 57 per cent of voters had heard of Labour's special conference at Wembley, at which the electoral college was established.

people with whom they should be in close contact. In such conditions, the party is vulnerable to infiltration, in a way in which a flourishing party with a large active membership is not. Additionally, if the group of active members is small, the machinery of the party is more open to manipulation. The Brightside case, justified as the party undoubtedly was in sacking its MP, showed how the party constitution could be a powerful weapon in the hands of those who know it well.

All of these considerations point in the direction of allowing a wider section of the party to take part in the selection and reselection procedures. While one may feel a certain sympathy with the argument that those who do all the hard work in the party should have some reward for their labours, choice of the candidate or MP seems a disproportionate prize. The 'skill' argument is a poor one; selections, at least in safe seats, are rare enough for many GMC members to take part in only one or two such choices in a lifetime of activism. It is also questionable when it is recalled that the selection process has quite frequently produced MPs whom the activists regard as unsatisfactory. Nor is it an argument which comes well from self-proclaimed anti-elitists. Most important is the argument that widening the field of selectors would increase the influence of the mass media. This is a dangerous line to take, as two prominent CLPD members have pointed out:

> It can be levelled with equal force against the universal franchise, the extension of participation in voting for the party leader outside the House of Commons, and mass meetings on the factory floor which decide on industrial action. (Frances Morrell and Brian Sedgemore, 'Setting Labour on the long road to Democracy', *Guardian* 26 November 1979).

What is more, those in favour of reselection have always maintained that one of its benefits would be a revival of party activity at grassroots level; the logical conclusion, then, is to extend participation to those grassroots.

But as Chapter 8 showed, reselection has raised fears of intolerance; just as some on the right of the party see accountability in a perspective which is too limited to include the rank and file of the party, some on the left seek not accountability, but subservience. The CLPD analysis of MPs' voting records, for example, appears to put undue pressure not only on MPs, but also perhaps on constituency parties. Reselection can be a method of improving accountability, but as the pamphlet itself declares, 'accountability is a two-way process, which confers responsibility on the party as well as the MP', and it should not be used to stifle every dissenting opinion. If it were to do so, Ostrogorski's worst fears would have been realised. Some of the behaviour of the groups with which the campaign has allied itself has gone against the 'tradition of civility and tolerance which is an essential part of our democracy' (Kogans, 1982, p. 142). The loss of MPs such as George Cunningham, who though reselected by his Islington constituency party, then became an Independent, is a blow to the party. If the critical scrutiny is relentless, and an MP is constantly at risk if he disagrees with the party leadership in the constituency, the question might seriously be asked whether anyone should want the job (Kogans, 1982, p. 140).

An MP is first and foremost a party man, but he is also the representative of and link with national politics of all those in the constituency, whether they voted for him or not. He must, on some issues, take a wider view than that of the party activists, because he represents not only them, but others as well. The Labour Party is a diverse party, and an MP must try and take account of that diversity; this would be facilitated by greater involvement of ordinary members.

What is required, then, is a method by which the greater accountability of MPs, as implied by the provisions for regular reselection, can be combined with greater participation for all members of the party. This would be similar in some respects to the primary elections which are used in most states in the USA. The introduction of primaries to Britain is now once more a fashionable proposal as a remedy for the increasing dissatisfaction with the workings of the two-party system; but it has been raised periodically over many years. Nigel Nicolson, for instance, succeeded in putting his candidacy to the whole membership of his local association, and this was called Britain's 'first primary election'. A similar procedure has also taken place in several cases of disputed selections in the Conservative Party. As a specific proposal for reform rather than in special cases, it has been put forward several times by MPs who had recurrent problems with their constituency parties.

Humphry Berkeley, then a Conservative, was one such. He had had continuous disagreements with the local association in his Lancaster constituency, on independence for colonial territories in Africa, on the abolition of capital punishment and on homosexual law reform. By introducing primaries, he argued, the field of selectors would be enlarged 'beyond the narrow range of committed party workers to all supporters within the constituency' (1968, p. 104). There would be two virtues in this; it would associate more closely the supporters of a particular party with the candidate for whom they would be asked to vote. It would also give the candidate (or MP) a body which was fully representative of support within the party to which he could appeal if a dispute arose with the Whips' office or the local executive committee.

Woodrow Wyatt, another MP who had difficulties with his constituency party, also proposed primaries, but he put more stress on the second aspect. Primaries, he thought, would 'stiffen the character of MPs',

> an immediate result of primaries would be that MPs would be far less
> subject, if subject at all, to the fanaticism of their local caucuses,
> either in their selection or during their time in Parliament (1973, p.
> 247).

Journalist Peter Paterson, another supporter of this idea, also took this view: they could provide for the MP 'a firm base against the old caucus which formerly could make or break him'. The aim of these proposals, although they all predate mandatory reselection, is clear – to give the MP a greater degree of independence in his relations with the constituency party. This does not necessarily mean that he would be freer; it might be that, in addition to the local party leadership, he would find that there were other groups and interests whose expectations he had to satisfy.

Other arguments in favour of primaries are that they might deal with some of the shortcomings of the selection procedure by bringing normally secret matters into the open. And ordinary party members would be enabled to choose between several representatives of their chosen party, rather than as at present being prevented from supporting the party while rejecting the candidate.

Since the proposals for primaries are inspired by the system in the United States, we should briefly examine the experience there. The system was introduced early in the twentieth century, with the aim of breaking the power of the caucuses. To a certain extent, it has been successful; but the influence of the party leaderships has been moderated rather than abolished. Most states have primaries for the nomination of both senators and congressmen, but the methods used vary widely. The majority of primaries are 'closed' ones, that is limited to registered party members, but in some states 'open' primaries are used, in which voters do not have to decide which party they wish to support until the day of the election. In theory, this can lead to members of one party voting in the other party's primary in an attempt to nominate the weakest candidate, a practice known as 'raiding'. Eleven southern states also use the 'run-off' primary. If the leading candidate in the initial primary fails to get a majority of votes, a second is held in which the choice is narrowed to the two candidates who came highest in the ballot. 'In one-party states, this system has the advantage that the person who gets the nomination – and hence wins the election – is guaranteed the support of more than just the small plurality that is often enough to win a race in which three or more strong candidates are seeking nomination' (Carr *et al.* 1963, p. 213). In the Democrat-dominated southern states, turnout figures are much higher for primaries than for the election proper. Many candidates are unopposed; a very rare occurrence in selections of British parliamentary candidates.

The caucus has a tendency to reassert itself. A 'narrowing of the scope' of the primary election as a result of the influence of the party organisation has taken place. This takes the form of a process known as 'slatemaking', which is a reversion to older methods. The stronger the party system in a state, the more likely it is that the party leadership will be effective in influencing the outcome of the primaries, which thus become a mere formality to elicit the consent of the voters. What happens is that the party leadership screens all potential candidates and selects, by a method which seems rather similar to selection in the Labour and Conservative parties, a candidate for each of the elective posts to be filled. This may involve 'a great deal of give-and-take between the candidates, their supporters and the party leaders'; once a slate has been agreed, the party then tries to ensure, by both negative and positive means, that the slate will be unopposed at the primary. 'If this is achieved, then no upsets are possible and the campaign resources of the party can be used sparingly so that major efforts can be concentrated on the opposition party in the general election.' (Sittig, 1967, p. 95.)

In order to prevent this by-passing of the general public, several states have introduced pre-primary conventions at which both the party leadership and the rank and file can express preferences. This has the advantage of allowing the party leadership to make their preferences clear from among the potential nominees, but also permits other candidates to appeal directly to the rank and file. 'It offers the voter a check on the leadership, while at the same time it recognises that party leaders are going to involve themselves in the nominating process regardless of the particular system that the law requires.' (Sittig, 1967, p. 97.)

Two obvious questions have exercised American academics and are relevant to any discussion about the usefulness of introducing primaries in Britain. The first is that of representativeness. Those who advocate them here usually feel that the party activists as opposed to the ordinary members are in some way unrepresentative. Might this also be true of people who vote in primaries? Two detailed studies of Wisconsin primaries show that those who vote in primaries are not in any way unrepresentative of those who do not. They are more active and involved, that is all. 'The active are unquestionably unrepresentative of the inactive. But can we expect anything else?' (Ranney and Epstein, 1966.)

A second problem which might arise is that of divisiveness. Does a hard-fought primary produce splits among the party's supporters? Are those who backed the loser keen to work for the winner in the election? Might uncommitted voters feel that a public fight of this kind renders the party unsuitable for public office? None of these appear to be the case, though there are likely to be adverse effects on the winner of a close-fought primary if the campaign has involved 'mudslinging' or if the winner has been accused of extremism.

What is clear from American experience, however, is the great advantage given to the incumbent in all primaries: the challengers usually have only a small hope of being nominated and the primary 'under those circumstances is of minimal effect in determining the party nominee for the general election' (Sittig, 1967, p. 94).

But as the foregoing discussion shows very clearly, the American party system is strikingly different from that in Britain. Parties are not 'responsible', they generally lack any strong national organisation, and they are not founded on any ideological or social basis. Indeed, they are completely heterogeneous: 'fundamentally they are organisations for the conquest of political and administrative offices, and for the nomination of candidates in "primaries" ' (Duverger, 1964, p. 210). Nor does membership of a party have any of the usual characteristics of membership of an association. Participation in a primary is the only activity typical of party membership. No subscriptions are paid, no meetings attended. So the party has no control over its membership; a person simply declares himself to be a member, and expulsion is not possible. In addition, many administrative as well as political posts are elective – hence the 'slates'; and there are a number of one-party areas.

Given these major differences between the two political systems and political cultures, American experience cannot be a very reliable guide to the effect of introducing primaries in Britain. But in the British party system, which demands a much higher level of commitment from party members, closed primaries might have a greater impact on candidate selection and could become something more than merely a matter of eliciting consent. Any reform would be unlikely to be a carbon-copy of American methods – themselves very diverse – as this would involve a fixed date for general elections. It would also involve legislation, and the agreement of the political parties, which is very improbable since such a change is opposed by both the Conservative and Labour parties. Up to now, British parties, unlike those in the USA, are untouched by the law so far as their internal operations are concerned.

What would be entirely possible, however, and as this chapter has tried to show, desirable, would be an internal reform by the Labour Party which would give a greater say to the rank and file of the party in the selection and reselection of parliamentary candidates. This would have a certain amount in common with a closed primary, and so American experience may provide a rough indication of what its effects might be.

Such a reform would restrict participation to the paid-up members of the party. Most proposals for primaries in Britain have favoured the closed primary; open primaries are vulnerable to raiding by outsiders, and a certain level of commitment is generally seen as essential. The Hansard

Society Report on electoral reform (1976), for example, argued that only those who 'have sufficient commitment actually to join a party' should take part. Exactly how the procedure would work is open to debate. The Hansard Society (proposing primaries) suggested a postal ballot. For the left wing this would give too much to passive members; selection and re-selection 'should demand more effort than posting a letter' (Wise, 1979). And indeed in ordinary elections of all kinds, postal ballots are available only in special cases. But there are also dangers to be discerned in a huge selection conference: skilful orators might be able to sway the voters too easily. Assuming that some sort of campaign took place, with the nominees addressing meetings in wards and union branches, the candidates' speeches and canvassing efforts could be separated from the voting itself as they are in parliamentary elections, and a secret ballot could be held in a similar way.

In this way the number of selectors could be increased – as noted in Chapter 3, at present most candidates are selected by as small a group as before the 1832 Reform Act – while at the same time recognising the important role of the party in the constituency, sustaining the candidate and MP and taking part in the national debate within the party on policy. The influence of the activists would be decreased; they would still have an important part in drawing up the shortlist of potential candidates, though regard would have to be paid to the views of ward and branch members. And as opinion formers, the 'energetic few' would no doubt have a good deal of influence on the less politically active. As J. S. Mill saw: 'One person with a belief is a social power equal to ninety-nine who have only interests' (1972, p. 186).

Whatever form the detailed arrangements might take, such a closed primary procedure should not give too much to the position of an incumbent MP. The aim of some of those who have promoted the idea has been to give the MP a stick with which to beat the local party's management committee. The Hansard Society Commission's proposal was that sitting MPs should be subject to a renomination procedure only if 20 per cent of the paid-up members of the party had signed a declaration to the effect that they required an election to be held. This is in effect a re-run of the Mikardo Compromise. But the implication of the primary proposal, even if in the USA many contenders are returned unopposed, is not only to enlarge the number of selectors but to widen the field of choice open to them. A rule that provided for at least two candidates in the primary should be acceptable to both sides of the party. The argument in 1981 over the question of a shortlist of one could just as easily have been reversed, with the left arguing in favour of only one name if the executive preferred it so, and the right calling, in the name of democracy, for a choice to be available.

Would the effect of a hard-fought primary be a divisive one on the local party? This is not generally found to be the case in the US, though American parties have no ideology like the Labour Party. In any case, the need to appeal to all members of the party would tend, though this is not demonstrable, to reduce both the importance of ideology and the attraction of candidates at either extreme.

What is more likely is that local party control would be increased at the expense of the centre. That this might be the effect of mandatory re-selection was predicted by Callaghan at the 1979 conference; he feared that it would 'weaken the central thrust that comes from common action'. Whether this will be the long-term effect of reselection remains to be seen. It is certainly the case that all MPs who have been removed in the re-selection process so far have been replaced by local men. Selection and re-selection by all the party members might strengthen this tendency. American experience of primaries indicates the likelihood of local issues becoming more important: 'It is extremely difficult to focus the attention of the voters on national issues' (Carr *et al.*, 1963, p. 214). In a much smaller, and still relatively homogeneous nation with strong national party leadership, this effect is likely to be less marked. But it might be welcome to the voters: the Granada Survey referred to in Chapter 3 brought out clearly that most voters put more stress on an MP's local responsibilities than on his parliamentary duties. '... constituents expect their Member to put local interests, and local opinion, before all else'. Expressing voters' concern about national issues and dealing with constituents problems were paramount. Electors want someone who will link them with the 'remote world of national politics' (Crewe, 1975, p. 321).

Although desirable for a variety of reasons, it cannot be claimed that such a change in the selection procedure would immediately remove all its faults. In particular, it would not reduce the parochial nature of many selections. As we have seen, few selection committees choose their candidate with any concept of the national interest in mind. Nor, with single-member constituencies, is there anything resembling the 'balanced ticket' so important to the American parties. Ethnic minorities have no represent-ation at all in the Commons, and women are poorly represented. Attempts to alter this require some form of positive discrimination, which is in effect an attempt to rig the system as it now stands. The CLPD has proposed this, and the draft constitution of the new SDP includes the provision that any parliamentary shortlist of three must include one woman and a list of six must include two.

One argument against increasing the number of selectors has been that if information on potential candidates is inadequate under the present system, opening it up to more participants might only make matters worse. This need not be the case; the contenders would have to present themselves effectively to the party members, and the campaign could be organised in such a way as to allow maximum information. Selections might become less the result of political manoeuvres within a small group. But most important of all, the introduction of this form of closed primary could keep open channels of communication between MPs, activists, and members, and prevent the party becoming a closed sect out of touch with wider Labour support.

There is evidence that reselection is a popular idea. One poll found that as many as 83 per cent of Labour supporters favoured it (Hodgson, 1981, p. 38). In another survey, a majority of voters of all parties thought it would be 'a good thing' (*The Times*, 9 February 1981). Although there has been an increasing tendency towards political apathy, the opportunity to participate might be eagerly seized. The success of pressure groups of all kinds, including tenants' associations, has shown that there is a willingness to take part. The EEC referendum, too, revealed the existence on both sides of the previously untapped reserves of enthusiasm for a political cause (Bogdanor, 1981, p. 66). The same may be concluded from the early successes of the SDP. If, as seems to be the case, there is a link between participation and a sense of political efficacy, a similar link may also exist between the partisan decline of recent years and cynicism about politicians and apathy (Crewe *et al.*, 1977). Altering the method of candidate selection in the Labour Party is not going to change this overnight, or on its own, but it could make a contribution towards tightening the bonds between party and society.

The virtues of this proposal may be seen as being considerably weakened by the fact that it comes from the right of the party. Some right-wingers have undergone 'Pauline conversions' (Frank Field, *The Times*, 20 February 1981) in favour of this version of party democracy. But this objection to it is as insubstantial as was opposition to greater democracy and accountability on the grounds that the campaign originated on the left of the party. Some such reform is essential if Labour is to meet the challenge of the Social Democrats, and equally if it is to resist the extreme left who have never had time for Parliament and who have no significant support in the electorate. As Professor Hobsbawm argued before Labour's 1981 Conference, there is no use having a left party if the masses do not vote for it. What is required is a broad party, not just a class party, still less a sectional pressure group or an alliance of minority interests, but a 'people's party'. This implies a recognition of diversity, not just in the party but within the country as a whole, a recognition, 'not only that the left and right, however embattled, belong to a broad movement, but that they both have a right to be there'. Further, it means thinking of politics not primarily in terms of activists, but in terms of ordinary people, 'people who remember the date of the Beatles' break-up and not the date of the

Saltley pickets; people who have never read *Tribune* and do not care a damn about the deputy leadership of the Labour party' (*Guardian*, 28 September 1981). These ordinary people have no sympathy with ideologies which are 'forever purifying themselves by separating off "tendencies" ' (Drucker, 1979, p. 68). Such exclusiveness is out of tune with the tolerance with which the party has been operated in the past, in spite of its deep divisions. That tolerance has been severely strained by the reselection issue, and the virtues of the reform would have been perverted if it were to become a means of purging all those with independent views.

The role of MPs was once again a major issue at the 1981 conference. Two resolutions were debated which aimed at democratising the procedures of the PLP. The theme of partnership between the parliamentarians and the rest of the party was stressed. Eric Heffer, replying for the NEC to a debate on a resolution which would have obliged MPs to sign a declaration that they would stand by the party programme, reminded his audience of his past rebellions, and said:

> We cannot tie down every individual to every Conference resolution . . . we have got to get this relationship right . . . we do not want the PLP to be puppets, but neither do we want the Conference resolutions to be ignored.

Michael Foot, too, defended the right of MPs to a measure of independence:

> The partnership has got to be one in which the parliamentary party does not presume the right to dictate to the party Conference, and the party Conference does not presume the right to dictate to the parliamentary party . . . we have got to show a spirit of tolerance.

He would, he said, never issue 'dog licences' to MPs, they must have the 'right to exercise their own judgement . . . their own political knowledge and experience – that must be part of our democracy too'.

These two statements recognise that there is no sovereign power in the party and admit some of the flaws in the workings of party government. They also recognise that the role of the MP is bound to be a problematic one. Prospects for a reform which would more closely involve ordinary party members are not bright, and the party remains split between parliamentarians and activists. But the political system as a whole is now, more than at any time in recent history, in a state of change. The mould may be about to break. Political allegiances are shifting, the two-party system is fast dissolving, and parliamentary discipline is faltering. In these circumstances, the position of MPs is likely to be more problematic, and perhaps more important than for many years. It is clear that the old ways of viewing an MP's role and representation as a whole, are no longer adequate. There is no single expression of that role which commands widespread acceptance. Here again, a recognition of diversity may be what is needed. But what will also be required is a greater recognition of the needs and wishes of ordinary voters, and closer links between the people and their elected representatives.

The view of representation put forward by such writers as the late Robert McKenzie put most of the emphasis on leadership. While admitting that the party leaders cannot 'ignore with impunity the moods and aspirations of their followers', he stresses the 'chain of responsibility from Cabinet to Parliament to electorate'. This stress was intended to disallow what he saw as undue influence by the rank and file on policy-making. And while we may accept some of his reservations about conference's role as a policy-making instrument, this view, – a 'realistic' one – sees the democratic process purely as a choice between competing teams of leaders:

> the mass parties are primarily the servants of their respective parliamentary parties; ... their principle function is to sustain teams of parliamentary leaders between whom the electorate is periodically invited to choose (1965, p. 647).

Thus democracy is only a method of choosing governments, rather than a kind of society. The ethical content of the concept, as set out by Mill and his followers is gone; there is no sense of democracy as a means of self-realisation through participation by ordinary people.

This realistic view is widely accepted, and indeed the parties have not only become victims of it, but have propagated it. But if we are to adapt our view of representation to suit the conditions of the late twentieth century, more stress must be put on participation and responsiveness. Consequently, though the ideas of Burke and the theory of party government both still have a certain relevance they are too simple. Today's MPs face a more complex world and must respond to electors who want more accountability and a closer connection between themselves and their representative. They find themselves serving more than one master; but this need not undermine the independence of the representative. As Lord Scarman wrote in another context, 'Consultation does not destroy independent judgement, it informs judgement'.

References and Further Reading

Aitken, Ian (1966) 'The structure of the Labour Party', in Kaufman (ed.).

Alderman, R.K. (1964–5) 'Discipline in the PLP 1945–51', *Parliamentary Affairs*, Vol. 18, pp. 293–305.

Alderman, R.K. (1965–6) 'The conscience clause of the Labour Party', *Parliamentary Affairs*, Vol. 19, pp. 224–232.

Alderman, R. K. (1967–8) 'Parliamentary party discipline in opposition: the parliamentary Labour Party 1951–64', *Parliamentary Affairs*, Vol. 21, pp. 124–136.

Allaun, Frank, Mikardo, Ian, and Sillars, Jim (1972) *Labour: Party or Puppet?*, Tribune Group.

Baldock, J. Unpublished paper on the Sheffield rent strike of 1967–8.

Barker, Ernest (1951) *Essays on Government*, 2nd edn., OUP, Chapter VI, 'Burke and his Bristol Constituency 1774–1780.'

Beer, Samuel (1957) 'The representation of interests in British government; historical background', *American Political Science Review*, Vol. 51, pp. 613–650.

Beer, Samuel (1965) *Modern British Politics*, Faber and Faber.

Benn, A.W. (1970) *The New Politics: a Socialist reconnaissance*, Fabian Tract no. 402.

Berkeley, Humphry (1968) *The Power of the Prime Minister*, Allen and Unwin.

Bilski, R. (1977) 'The Common Market and the growing strength of Labour's left wing', *Government and Opposition*, Vol. 12, no. 3, pp. 306–331.

Bing, Inigo (ed.) (1971) *The Labour Party: an Organisational Study*, Fabian Tract no. 407.

Birch A.H. (1964) *Representative and Responsible Government*, Allen and Unwin.

Birch A.H. (1972) *Representation*, Macmillan.

Birch A.H. (1977) *Political Integration and Disintegration in the British Isles*, Allen and Unwin.

Birch A.H. (1980) *The British System of Government*, 4th edn., Allen and Unwin.

Bogdanor, Vernon (1981) *The People and the Party System*, CUP.

Butler, David (1978) 'The Renomination of MPs: a note', *Parliamentary Affairs*, Vol. 31, pp. 210–212.

Butler, David and Kavanagh, Dennis (1980) *The British General Election of 1979*, Macmillan.

Butler, David and Pinto-Duschinsky, Michael (1971) *The British General Election of 1970*, Macmillan.

Butler, David and Rose, Richard (1960) *The British General Election of 1959*, Macmillan.

Butt, Ronald (1967), *The Power of Parliament*, Constable.

Carr, Robert K., Bernstein, Marver H. and Murphy, Walter F. (1963) *American Democracy in Theory and Practice*, 4th edn.

Coates, David (1975) *The Labour Party and the Struggle for Socialism*, CUP.

Coates, David (1980) *Labour in Power?*, Longman.

Coates, Ken (1973) 'Socialists and the Labour Party', *Socialist Register*.

Conniff, James (1977) 'Burke, Bristol and the concept of representation', *Western Political Quarterly*, pp. 329–341.

Cook, Chris and Ramsden, John (1973) *By-Elections in British Politics*, Macmillan.

Crewe, Ivor (1975) 'Electoral reform and the local MP', in Finer (ed.).

Crewe, Ivor and Spence, James (1973) 'Parliament and public', *New Society*, 12 July.

Crewe, Ivor, Särlvik, Bo and Alt, James (1977) 'Partisan de-alignment in Britain 1964–74', *British Journal of Political Science*, part II, Vol. 7, pp. 129–190.

Crossman, R. H. S. (1963) Introduction to Bagehot's *English Constitution*, Fontana.

Crossman, R. H. S. (1976, 1977) *Diaries of a Cabinet Minister*, Vols. II and III, Hamish Hamilton and Cape.

Dickson, A. D. R. (1975) 'MPs' readoption conflicts: their causes and consequences', *Political Studies*, Vol. 23, pp. 62–70.

Dickson, A. D. R. (1979) Unpublished Ph.D thesis on readoption conflicts, Paisley College of Technology.

Dowse, Robert (1963) 'The MP and his surgery', *Political Studies*, Vol. 11, pp. 333–341.

Dowse, Robert and Smith, Trevor (1962–3) 'Party discipline in the House of Commons: a comment', *Parliamentary Affairs*, Vol. 16, pp. 159–164.

Drucker, H. M. (1979) *Doctrine and Ethos in the Labour Party*, Allen and Unwin.

Duverger, Maurice (1964) *Political Parties*, 3rd. edn., Faber.

Eulau, Heinz, Wahlke, John C., Buchanan, William and Ferguson, Leroy C. (1959) 'The role of the representative: some empirical observations on the theory of Edmund Burke', *American Political Science Review*, Vol. 53, pp. 742–756.

Finer, S. E. (ed.) (1975a) *Adversary Politics and Electoral Reform*, Anthony Wigram.

Finer, S. E. (1975b) 'Manifesto Moonshine', *New Society*, 13 November.

Finer, S. E. (1980) *The Changing British Party System 1945–1979*, American Enterprise Institute.

Foot, Paul (1968) *The Politics of Harold Wilson*, Penguin.

Forester, Tom (1973) 'Anatomy of a Local Labour Party', *New Statesman*, 5 October.

Forester, Tom (1976) *The Labour Party and the Working Class*, Heinemann.

Gwyn, W. B. and Rose, Richard (eds.) (1980) *Britain: Progress and Decline*, Macmillan.

Hacker, Andrew (1965) 'Does a "Divisive" Primary harm a Candidate's chances?'*American Political Science Review*, Vol. 59, pp. 105–110.

Hampton, William (1970) *Democracy and Community: a study of Politics in Sheffield*, OUP.

Hansard Society (1976) *Report of Commission on Electoral Reform*.

Harrison, Reginald (1980) *Pluralism and Corporatism*, Allen and Unwin.

Heffer, Eric (1972) 'Labour's future', *Political Quarterly*, Vol. 43, pp. 380–388.

Hill, B. W. (1975) *Edmund Burke on Government, Politics, and Society*, Fontana.

Hodgson, Geoff (1981) *Labour at the Crossroads*, Martin Robertson.

Hindess, Barry (1971) *The Decline of Working Class Politics*, MacGibbon and Kee.

Houghton, Douglas (1972) 'Making MPs accountable', *Political Quarterly*, Vol. 43, pp. 375–379.

Ionescu, Ghita (1975a) *Centripetal Politics*, Hart Davis, MacGibbon.

Ionescu, Ghita (1975b) 'The shrinking world of Bagehot', *Government and Opposition*, Vol. 10, pp. 1–11.

Jackson, Robert (1975) *Rebels and Whips*, Macmillan.

Janosik, E. G. (1968) *Constituency Labour Parties in Britain*, Praeger.

Jeger, L. (1968) 'The grass comes away from the roots', *New Statesman*, 5 April.

Johnson, Nevil (1977) *In Search of the Constitution*, Pergamon Press.

Judge, David (1981) *Backbench Specialisation in the House of Commons*, Heinemann Educational Books.

Kavanagh, Dennis (1970) *Constituency Electioneering in Britain*, Longmans.

Kavanagh, Dennis (1978) 'New bottles for new wines', *Parliamentary Affairs*, Vol. 31, pp. 6–21.

Kaufman, Gerald (ed.) (1966) *The Left*, Blond.

King, Anthony (1975) 'Overload: the problems of governing in the 1970s', *Political Studies*, Vol. 23, pp. 288–296.

Kogan, David and Kogan, Maurice (1982) *The Battle for the Labour Party*, Fontana.

Labour Party Annual Conference Reports (1960–1981).

Lazer, Harry (1976) 'British populism: the Labour Party and the Common Market parliamentary debate', *Political Science Quarterly*, Vol. 91, pp. 259–277.

Layton-Henry, Z. (1979) 'Reforming the Labour Party', *Political Quarterly*, pp. 435–444.

Lever, Harold (1981) 'Accountability', *London Review of Books*, 19 March – 1 April.

McCallum, R. B. and Redman, A. (1947) *The British General Election of 1945*, Macmillan.

McCormick, Paul (1979) *Enemies of Democracy*, Temple Smith.

McKenzie, Robert (1963) *British Political Parties*, 2nd. edn., Heinemann.

McKie, David, Cook, Chris and Phillips, Melanie (1979) *Guardian Quartet Election Guide*, Quartet.

Mackintosh, J. (1972) 'Socialism or social democracy? The choice for the Labour Party', *Political Quarterly*, Vol. 43, no. 4, pp. 470–484.

Mackintosh, J. P. (ed.) (1978) *People and Parliament*, Saxon House.

Macpherson, C. B. (1977) *The Life and Times of Liberal Democracy*, OUP.

Macpherson, C. B. (1980) *Burke*, OUP.

Marquand, David (1979) 'Inquest on a movement', *Encounter*, July.

Marquand, David (1981) Article in *London Review of Books*, 1–14 October.

Martin, Laurence W. (1960) 'The Bournemouth affair: Britain's first primary election', *Journal of Politics*, pp. 654–681.

Miliband, Ralph (1958) 'Party democracy and parliamentary government', *Political Studies*, Vol. 6, no. 3, pp. 170–174.

Miliband, Ralph (1961) *Parliamentary Socialism*, Merlin Press.

Mill, John Stuart (1972) *Considerations on Representative Government*, Everyman.

Milne, Eddie (1976) *No Shining Armour*, Calder.

Minkin, Lewis (1974) 'The British Labour Party and the trade unions: crisis and compact', *Industrial and Labour Relations Review*, Vol. 28, October pp. 7–37.

Minkin, Lewis (1978a) 'The Party Connection', *Government and Opposition*, Vol. 13, no. 4, pp. 458–484.

Minkin, Lewis (1978b) *The Labour Party Conference*, Allen Lane.

Morrell, Frances (1977) *From the Electors of Bristol*, Spokesman pamphlet no. 57.

Mullin, Chris (1981) *How to Select or Reselect your MP*, Campaign for Labour Party Democracy/Institute for Workers' Control.

Munroe, Ronald (1977) 'The member of Parliament as representative: the view from the constituency', *Political Studies*, Vol. 25, pp. 577–587.

Newman, R., and Cranshaw, S. (1973) 'Towards a closed primary election in Britain', *Political Quarterly*, Vol. 44, no. 4, pp. 447–452.

Nicolson, Nigel (1958) *People and Parliament*, Weidenfeld and Nicolson.

Ostrogorski, M. (1964, first published 1902) *Democracy and the Organisation of Political Parties*, (edited and abridged by S. M. Lipset), Doubleday/Anchor Books.

Owen, David (1981) *Face the Future*, Jonathan Cape.

Paterson, Peter (1967) *The Selectorate*, MacGibbon and Kee.

Pennock and Chapman (eds.) (1968) *Representation*, Atherton Press.

Pennock and Chapman (eds.) (1975) *Participation in Politics*, Lieber-Atherton.

Pateman, Carole (1970) *Participation and Democratic Theory*, CUP.

Phillips Griffiths, A. (1960) 'How can one person represent another?' Aristotelian Society *Proceedings*, Supp. Vol. pp. 187–208.

Pitkin, Hanna (1967) *The Concept of Representation*, University of California Press.

Radice, Giles and Lapping, Brian (eds.) (1968) *More Power to the People*, Longmans.

Ranney, Austin (1965) *Pathways to Parliament*, Macmillan.

Ranney, A. (1968) 'The representativeness of primary electorates', *Midwest Journal of Political Science*, Vol. 12, no. 2, pp. 224–238.

Ranney, A. and Epstein L. (1966) 'The two electorates: voters and non-voters in a Wisconsin primary', *Journal of Politics*, Vol. 28, no. 3, pp. 598–616.

Richards, P. G. (1959) *Honourable Members*, Faber.

Richards, P. G. (1980) *Parliament and Conscience*, Allen and Unwin.

Roberts, E. (1972) 'Trade unions and the Labour Party', *Labour Monthly*, May, pp. 207–210.

Rose, Paul (1981) *Backbencher's Dilemma*, Muller.

Rose, Richard (1976) *The Problem of Party Government*, Penguin.

Rose, Richard (1980) *Do Parties Make a Difference?*, Macmillan.

Roth, Andrew (1971) *Can Parliament Decide?*, MacDonald.

Rush, Michael (1969) *The Selection of Parliamentary Candidates*, Nelson.

Seyd, Patrick (1974) 'The Tavernite', *Political Quarterly*, Vol. 45, pp. 242–246.

Seyd, Patrick (1978) 'Fighting for the soul of the Labour Party', *New Society*, 20 April.

Seyd, Patrick and Minkin, Lewis (1979) 'The Labour Party and its Members', *New Society*, 20 September.

Sittig, R. (1967) 'The direct primary: permanent decline or temporary eclipse?', *Social Science*, Vol. 42, no. 2, pp. 94–98.

Smith, Trevor (1979) *The Politics of the Corporate Economy*, Martin Robertson.

Taverne, Dick (1974) *The Future of the Left*, Jonathan Cape.

Telford, I. R. (1965) 'Types of primary and party responsibility', *American Political Science Review*, Vol. 59, no. 1, pp. 117–118.

Turner, John (1978) *Labour's Doorstep Politics in London*, Macmillan.

Ware, Alan (1979) 'Divisive primaries: the important questions', *British Journal of Political Science*, Vol. 9, part 3, pp. 381–384.

Williams, Shirley (1981) *Politics is for People*, Allen Lane.

Wilson, Harold (1971) *The Labour Government 1964–70: A Personal Record*, Weidenfeld/Joseph.

Wilson, Harold (1979) *Final Term: the Labour government 1974–76*, Weidenfeld/Joseph.

Wise, Audrey (1979) 'Reselection: there is no case for giving special privilege to the non-attenders', *Tribune*, 23 November.

Wolin, S. S. (1961) *Politics and Vision*, Allen and Unwin.

Wyatt, Woodrow (1973) *Turn Again, Westminster*, Deutsch.

Index